# Guglielmo Marconi

by Beverley Birch

**OTHER TITLES IN THE SERIES**
Charles Darwin by Anna Sproule (1-85015-213-6)
Thomas A. Edison by Anna Sproule (1-85015-201-2)
Alexander Fleming by Beverley Birch (1-85015-184-9)
*Coming soon:*
Alexander Graham Bell by Michael Pollard (1-85015-200-4)
Galileo Galilei by Michael White (1-85015-227-6)
Margaret Mead by Anna Sproule (1-85015-228-4)
The Wright Brothers by Anna Sproule (1-85015-229-2)

**Picture Credits**
Bell Canada: 6; The Mary Evans Picture Library: 20, 44 both, 48; Exley Publications Photo Library,
Nick Birch: 29, 32 top, 36, 40, 54; Giancarlo Costa: 50, 55; Robert Harding: 9, 58 below, 59, 60;
The Image Bank (Frank Whitney): 58 left; The Marconi Company: 10, 30, 39, 47, 52; Moro Roma:
43; Rex Features: 4 (Peter Nelson); The Science Photo Library: 8 (Adam Hart), 12-3 (Gordon
Garrard), 16 & 17 (Vaughan Fleming), 24 right (Michael Burgess), 24 left (G. Hadjro, CNRI), 26
(Alex Bartel), 32 below (Phil Jude); Roger-Viollet: 23, 57; Zefa: 25.

Published in Great Britain in 1990
by Exley Publications Ltd,
16 Chalk Hill, Watford,
Herts WD1 4BN, United Kingdom.

**British Library Cataloguing in Publication Data**
Birch, Beverley.
   Guglielmo Marconi – (Scientists
   who have changed the world).
   1.   Radio. Marconi, Guglielmo, marchese.
        Fleming, Sir Alexander, *1881-1955*.
   I.   Title.
   II.  Series.
   621.3841'092'4

**ISBN 1-85015-185-7**

**Series conceived and edited by Helen Exley.**
Picture research: Elizabeth Loving.
Editorial: Margaret Montgomery.
Editorial Production: Samantha Armstrong.
Typeset by Brush Off Studios,
St Albans, Herts AL3 4PH.
Printed and bound in Spain by
Cronion SA, Barcelona.

# Guglielmo Marconi

*The story of radio and how it made the world a smaller place*

## Beverley Birch

⧉ EXLEY

# The hill at Villa Grifone

The young man waited, anxious, at the attic window. He threw a last look at the crest of the hill. Then he tapped a small metal lever mounted on a board in front of him, carefully. Once, twice, three times ...

A single shot echoed across the vineyards, high over hills and fields toward him ...

Success! At the speed of light the signal from his machine in the attic had sped to his brother down the valley. His brother had caught the vibrations from the air and with the joyful crack of his rifle he hailed his success!

Months of patient work had brought him to this moment. But now, with absolute certainty, he knew it was only the beginning. Scientists who knew much more than he did, thought he would not get even this far.

He had defied their predictions. He *had* sent a signal through the air, further than they dreamed possible. No wires connected his sending machine to the receiver. Trees, farm buildings, the great mound of the hill had not stopped the signal flowing.

Scientists would be even more doubtful that he could go any further.

But the young man had conceived an unshakeable conviction. The rifle shot told him he was right. One day ... one day he would link the countries of the world with such signals. One day, such a signal would wing its way from one end of the world to the other.

*Opposite: Rescue at sea. Before Marconi developed his wireless (radio) ships could call for help only if they could be <u>seen</u> from land or other ships. Marconi's wireless gave people the new chance to communicate with each other across vast distances <u>without</u> visual or physical links between them. Since the first Marconi wireless call for help at sea in 1899, radio has saved countless lives in land, sea and air rescue.*

5

*Telegraph and telephone wires in the United States in 1890. By the time Marconi learned of the new scientific discoveries that prompted his work on wireless, such networks of telegraph wires linked places all over Europe and the United States. The two were joined by the massive telegraph cable beneath the Atlantic Ocean. But all this communication depended on wires linking the sender and receiver of messages.*

## Cables around the world

It was a vast ambition that he had, and one that most people of his time believed was in the realms of science fiction.

This was the year 1895 – exciting times, for year by year scientists brought new transformations in our understanding of the world. The use of electricity was still quite new. Only over the last hundred years had scientists and inventors learned to produce it in a usable form. Only over the last sixty years had they begun to send messages by electric telegraph, and then, later, to drive industrial machines with it. Only in the last fourteen years had people used it widely for lighting in the home.

Gone were the days when messages had to be carried physically – by runners on foot or horseback, by ships across the oceans, and, later, by train. By 1895 the new science of electricity could send messages fast and accurately – by telegraph or telephone – along a wire. Between the sender of the message and the receiver there had to be a wire, for along this the electricity flowed.

Many scientists were trying to do it *without* wires. Some had managed to pass electricity through earth or water, and had succeeded over a few miles. They used no *connecting* wire between sender and receiver, but vast lengths of wire had to lie *parallel* to each other on opposite sides of the transmitting distance. More wire was needed on each side than the distance between them!

And signals sent like this went only a short way. The only reliable method, the only one that would travel any distance, was along a *connecting* wire.

By 1895, numerous cables had been laid under the seas – including the great Atlantic cable. Messages streamed along these as a flow of electricity. The telegraph operators used Morse code: each letter of the alphabet translated into its own pattern of dots and dashes. They sent these racing along the cable as short and long flows of electricity, by switching the electricity on and off.

All such communication relied upon a heavy, durable cable carrying the wires, physically laid and carefully maintained beneath or above the earth, or along the bottom of the seas.

*"My chief trouble was that the idea was so elementary, so simple in logic that it seemed difficult to believe no one else had thought of putting it into practice. In fact Oliver Lodge had, but he had missed the correct answer by a fraction. The idea was so real to me that I did not realize that to others the theory might appear quite fantastic."*
Guglielmo Marconi.

## Marconi's dream

The dream of the young man in the attic was quite different. His vision was of messages vibrating through the air, across vast distances. His signals would be hampered by no barrier – no mountain or ocean, no forest or lake. They would need no physical link between sender and receiver. And his signals would travel at the speed of light – three hundred thousand kilometres a second.

He was twenty when he conceived this dream. By the age of twenty-three, he had done it. And the electrical vibrations he sent first across those Italian fields around his home would one day reach satellites orbiting our earth in outer space, and then flow back again.

In his time they were known as wireless. We know them as radio.

## For those in peril

Countless people owe their lives to this vision of the young man Guglielmo Marconi. Wireless has given ships at sea, aircraft in the air, communities in the remotest parts of our globe, their vital links with the rest of the world. Even in its infancy, wireless would time and again save lives, for at the speed of light it could summon help to those who had always been beyond its reach.

The work of Guglielmo Marconi stands four-square as the gateway to the radio and television age. From his early wireless flowed all those developments we now take for granted – instant communication between people without physical link between them. However remote their position, wherever they may be moving, contact can be made if they have radio. Emergency, rescue and security services of the modern world spring from its powers. And from that early wireless we have inherited the broadcast entertainment we receive so directly in our homes – radio and television at the push of a button and the turn of a dial.

## Built upon the earliest pioneers

But the story of wireless is far more than the story of Guglielmo Marconi. His work was built firmly upon the brilliance of many others' previous researches.

In his system he combined and developed inventions that were the fruits of others' ingenuity over scores of years. He adapted them to his vision. He drew other scientists into the work he had begun, to design and build the great Marconi installations, to add their inventions to his.

It is to Marconi, however, that we owe that first great vision transformed to a practical reality – scientific principles applied to give the world a tool of immeasurable richness. In doing so, he lit a fire of excitement about wireless among scientists and inventors around the world.

Within thirty years the transformation begun by the twenty-year-old youth in the attic had brought the world-wide links he had dreamed about.

*Opposite: A radiotelescope – one of the many modern uses of radio. This kind studies sections of the sky, using a large dish "reflector" to detect radio waves that occur in outer space.*

*Below: The highest radio aerial in the world. It was Marconi's invention of aerials in 1895 that produced his workable communication system over long distances. Since then many different types of aerial have been designed, tailor-made to suit different kinds of radio wave. In all these developments, Marconi played a central role.*

## Childhood in Italy

Guglielmo Marconi was born on April 25, 1874, of an Irish mother and an Italian father, in the ancient Italian city of Bologna. But he grew up on his father's country estate in the hills seventeen kilometres from Bologna. Here, in the house known as Villa Grifone, he began what was to be his life's work.

Guglielmo's father, Giuseppe, inherited Villa Grifone and its estate from his own father. He was already fifty when Guglielmo was born, and among his fields and vineyards, raising silkworms and browsing in his library, he was happiest.

The villa perched on a hill above the village of Pontecchio. Fields fell to a fertile plain below, and beyond rose the ridges of the Appenine Mountains which run like a backbone down Italy. Behind the house, on the far side of a hill, stretched the vineyards.

Yet Guglielmo's Irish mother, Annie, seventeen years younger than his father, was restless spending the whole year on the estate. She took every opportunity to travel. Wanderings with his mother were a large part of Guglielmo's childhood. He was only three when he first visited relatives in England, the country where he would spend the greater part of his working life, and become world famous.

## Love of the sea

From his earliest years Annie always took Guglielmo and his brother Alfonso, nine years older, south in the winter.

Annie particularly liked the port of Leghorn, on the west coast of Italy. Her sister lived there with four daughters – good friends to Guglielmo and Alfonso. Guglielmo was very fond of the youngest of his cousins, Daisy, and he loved Leghorn, for at Leghorn, there was the sea.

Leghorn was the main port of central Italy. Here, the navy of Italy, the *Regia Marina*, had its academy. The inner port bobbed with craft carrying supplies for warships anchored in the bay. Sailors and

*Marconi with his Irish-born mother, Annie. His mother supported him staunchly throughout his early efforts in science.*

officers in their spanking uniforms came ashore. So much for a child to watch and dream about!

Guglielmo Marconi's love of the sea remained with him all his life: the sea would become his greatest laboratory for wireless, and his dearest retreat. Wireless for those at sea formed a central core in all his ambitions.

Guglielmo's father, Giuseppe, wanted him to become a naval officer and study for entrance to the naval academy. He even bought Guglielmo a sailing boat – and Giuseppe never spent money lightly. Guglielmo learned to sail the small craft expertly, and he loved to show off, nipping his little boat around the port.

But his father's ambitions for the academy were to be thwarted by another side of Guglielmo's nature. Much as he was fascinated by the sea, Guglielmo was also very bad at school work. He never spent time on things that he found boring.

## A bad student

His early education had all been at home at Villa Grifone, Leghorn and Florence. His parents employed a schoolmaster to make the boys fluent in Italian and give them steady education during the endless movement between Villa Grifone and winter months in warmer resorts. But Guglielmo was not an easy pupil. He did not like school work under this teacher and often stayed away, absorbed with other things he thought more important.

Guglielmo's first experience of formal school, at the age of twelve, was no better. It was in Florence. The other boys found him reserved, and were put off by his foreign ways, a legacy from his time in England and his mother and English cousins. The teachers found him backward in his studies and unapproachable: he was often in trouble for poor work.

Yet here Guglielmo made one of the most important friends of his life. Luigi Solari was one of the older pupils there. He liked the younger, rather stern-faced boy, for he saw through the unfriendly expression to the shyness and worry that hid

*Lightning in the sky. Electricity has been studied since the sixteenth century, but it was not until 1752 that Benjamin Franklin showed lightning was another form of the same force. Another half century passed before the battery was invented – which led to the ways in which we use electricity today.*

beneath. Their friendship would never cease. Luigi Solari was to help Marconi at several critical stages of his wireless work, and would be with him fifty years later, when he died.

## A fascination for science

For all his backwardness in school work, Guglielmo Marconi had no lack of interest in things he thought worthwhile. Even when very young he liked to escape to his father's library, to lose himself in

the books there – fascinated by the history of the Ancient Greeks and their great myths.

But as he grew older, stories and lectures of the scientists claimed his undivided attention.

Guglielmo had always been interested in the way things were put together – ever since he had wrestled with his first toys. Before he was ten he was forever concocting some gadget he had read about. Somewhere in the rambling Villa or farm buildings he would ferret out the things he needed – to bedeck the walls with wires and battery for an electric bell, to transform cousin Daisy's sewing machine into a turnspit for roasting meat ...

Daisy wept. Guglielmo transformed the turnspit back into Daisy's sewing machine. He talked proudly to her about "my electricity". She understood little, but admired greatly.

Not much older, Guglielmo and a friend in Leghorn erected a spear-like contraption made of zinc on the roof, and connected it to an electric bell inside the house. The plan was to catch electricity from a storm on the "spear". Then it would flow down the linking wire and ring the bell. Desperate days went by, the boys praying for bad weather. And when lightning flashed the bell *did* tinkle ...!

## War with his father

But it brought Guglielmo into bitter conflict with his father. Giuseppe Marconi could see nothing but dabbling and time-wasting in these "games". They merely frittered away hours better employed on school work.

There came the day when Guglielmo tried to copy an experiment done by the American scientist, Benjamin Franklin. He was one of the pioneers of electricity over a hundred years before, and one of Guglielmo's heroes.

His father saw only Guglielmo succeeding in smashing a large number of dinner plates in full view of passers-by. It was madness. And the madness must be stamped out. He set out to stop all his son's experiments and destroy any "contraptions" he found.

But Guglielmo Marconi had a staunch ally – his mother, Annie. From this time on, mother and son plotted to keep Guglielmo's "contraptions" from the disapproving eyes of father.

## Failure

His father's disappointment was confirmed when Guglielmo failed to get into the Naval Academy in Leghorn. He simply did not get the qualifications needed for a place there. Here was absolute proof for Giuseppe: these "scientific experiments" were idiotic rubbish. Guglielmo, encouraged by his mother, had squandered time he could never win back, time when he should have studied for a profession.

Guglielmo's own disappointment was deep, though well-hidden. What was he to do with his life? He was thirteen. For as long as he could remember he had wanted to go to the Naval Academy. Instead, in the winter of that year, 1887, he went to the Leghorn Technical Institute. To the father, and at first to the son, this was a poor alternative to the glory of a life in the Navy.

But in the Technical Institute, Guglielmo Marconi had entered a world that would finally capture him and harness his restless, searching intelligence.

## Lessons in science

Here he began to study physics and chemistry. Within days he was utterly absorbed. Here was the missing focus for all those years of playing with science. Here – in the study of the natural world, of what it is made of and what forces are at work in it – the thirteen-year-old boy at last found his place.

Annie saw her son in the grip of a real fascination. He could spare no time from reading or testing it out. More and more of his father's reluctantly-given money was siphoned off for Guglielmo's experiments. She struggled to keep the balance between her son's enthusiasm and anything his father could interpret as more hare-brained frittering of time and money. She realized that lectures at the institute were not enough to satisfy his curiosity and arranged for him to have extra lessons, privately.

## The pioneers of electricity

In the beginning Guglielmo read everything he could find about the burgeoning new science of electricity. He delved into great volumes about the earliest knowledge: how the Ancient Greeks

*A rare picture of young Marconi around the time he was developing his first radio apparatus at Villa Grifone.*

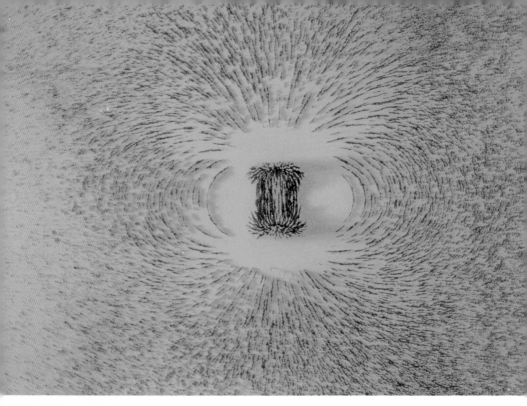

*Two examples of how a magnet affects metal. Above, loose iron filings scattered at random on paper, at once arrange themselves in patterns around a bar magnet held below the paper. Right, loose iron filings are attracted on to the bar magnet, building up extraordinary shapes.*

noticed that amber rubbed with fur attracted light objects. They believed it was because amber took on an invisible fluid. Their word for amber was *elektron* – from this we have the word electricity.

There were other observations by people in the ancient world, the earliest records in China around 2600 BC. They knew, for example, about *natural magnets* – lumps of metallic ore which could attract other metals to them. Just as intriguing was the fact that, if left to move freely, they always took up a position pointing north. This gave them their name of "lodestone", meaning "leading stone".

He read, too, of the earliest use of this knowledge – in the sailors' compasses, and then of the more systematic investigations that had been going on over the past three hundred years. One by one critical facts were discovered by different experimenters …

Turning the pages of the volumes, tracing the quest for understanding through the centuries, Guglielmo was amazed at the ingenuity of those

who had built the knowledge, observation by observation, experiment by experiment from tiny beginnings.

There were, these experimenters discovered, many substances that you could rub and so give them the ability to attract lighter objects. Gemstones, glass, resin, fossils – rub them with a piece of fur or cloth and they would attract feathers, paper ...

Even more fascinating, this mysterious force would pass from one thing to another. Sometimes it leapt through the air as a spark. It passed easily through some substances, like metals and water, but not through others, like silk, dry glass or air. By the early eighteenth century one scientist managed to lead electricity all around his garden and back again, on a kind of twine, held up by silk loops.

Then in 1752, Guglielmo Marconi's hero, Benjamin Franklin, showed that this electricity was a small relation of the violent flash of lightning in the sky.

## Sparks all the rage

For a time then electricity was all the rage. Scientists developed elaborate spark-making machines that rubbed one substance against another. Often they were a glass ball, rubbed with cloth. Royalty and fashionable society were much amused by contraptions that made people jump with electric shocks.

It was logical for someone to try to store this extraordinary force. Several succeeded almost at the same time – and the device known as a "Leyden jar" was invented. Originally it was glass on the outside (through which electricity would *not* flow easily), and metal on the inside (through which electricity *would* flow easily).

Into this container scientists could lead electricity with a wire, (they called it "charging" the jar) and hold it, until it was led out again – or *discharged*. And still the electricity for all this was supplied by some form of "continuous rubbing" or *friction* machine.

Exciting effects: but all sparks were over in an instant, and not yet much use, except for the fascination of it.

## Volta's battery

With excitement, Guglielmo learned that the next jump in knowledge came through the work of two of his countrymen. In 1800, an Italian scientist named Alessandro Volta invented the electric battery. It began in 1786, when Luigi Galvani, a scientist at the University of Bologna, noticed that a dead frog's leg twitched if he touched it *at the same time* with two wires – one of copper, the other of zinc.

It took some years before Volta realized what this really meant – that two *different* metals separated by *any* moist substance would produce a *continuous flow of electricity* – what we call an "electric current".

At first Volta used wet paper stacked vertically between metal plates. Then he developed batteries made of a series of cells containing liquid chemicals, linked by different metals – usually copper and zinc plates in a dilute acid. The more cells linked together, the more powerful the battery.

His invention caused a sensation throughout the scientific world. Within weeks it was being used to open new doors in scientific knowledge. As soon as scientists knew how to produce a *continuous flow of electricity* they could begin the long series of experiments that moved it out of the laboratory and into industry and the home.

All this Guglielmo absorbed with gusto. By the time he was sixteen, he had built his own machine for producing and transmitting electricity.

*"He [Marconi] was fond of both riding and rowing, at both of which he was very good; but he did not like sports, and he did not really want to play with other boys. A great deal of the time he spent hidden away in a secluded corner of the garden with an old jam-jar of water and a few strands of wire and odds and ends, working out some new experiment."*
Norman Wymer, from "Guglielmo Marconi".

## Another failure for Guglielmo

Once again there was big disappointment ahead. When the time came, Guglielmo Marconi failed the exam to get a place at the University of Bologna. Annie alone understood the depths of his misery. She was determined he should continue his studies.

By good fortune, one of the professors at the University of Bologna lived near the Villa Grifone. By an extra stroke of good fortune, he was Professor Augusto Righi, internationally acclaimed for the quality of his research and brilliance of his lectures on just the subject that fascinated Guglielmo – physics.

There was little evidence of Guglielmo's skills in physics to show Righi. But the professor must have been persuaded by the enthusiasm of the mother, for he began to allow the boy occasional use of his own laboratory and gave him access to the university library.

Guglielmo lost no time. He dived back into his studies. He had moved on, and was reading everything he could find about how electricity was being applied.

## Communications across the world

The university library was full of tales of the struggle to lay the electric telegraph across the world. There was something about this idea of world-wide communication that seized the boy's imagination. The scale of the effort! The subtlety of ideas, and the

*Laying the telegraph cable across the Atlantic Ocean. There were many failures before it was finally achieved in 1866, with the vast steamship the "Great Eastern" carrying the huge length of cable needed to stretch more than three thousand kilometres beneath the Ocean. Maintaining this cable in working order along its whole length was an equally marathon task.*

sheer persistence of the scientists!

Little did he know that slowly he was assembling the parts of a gigantic jigsaw he alone would solve.

By the 1890s, telegraph wires already crisscrossed Europe and the United States, underground or lifted in the air on posts. These two great networks were joined with the massive Atlantic cable. Guglielmo read of the marathon struggle to lay it – the many failed attempts and many years of work before they succeeded in 1866.

All these cables had to be maintained, repaired, new cables laid to extend the links ... Guglielmo's mind fluttered over the idea of a wire*less* kind of communication. He speculated, briefly, then on with his reading....

The first telegraphs used magnetic needles moved by an electric current to point to letters of the alphabet on a dial. But by now, in the 1890s, they used the Morse code instead.

# Morse code

Guglielmo Marconi's interest in Morse telegraphy had been spiced when he made friends in Leghorn with an old man, Nello Marchetti, who had once been an electric telegraph operator. Now he was going blind, and Guglielmo read to him.

Marchetti soon discovered the boy's fascination for the telegraph and set out to teach him the Morse code. He explained how a small lever (the Morse key) was pressed; this made an electric current flow along a wire, depending on how long you held the key down. At the other end, these electrical impulses were translated into long and short clicks or buzzer sounds, or printed on a Morse writer as dots and dashes. By the time Marchetti had finished, Guglielmo knew how to tap out the letters of the alphabet on a telegraphist's key.

Piece by piece, the parts of the puzzle, yet unrecognized, took firmer shape before him. Everything was preparing him for that day, in the summer of 1894, when he first read about the electrical waves that vibrated through space.

*"It seemed to me that if the radiation could be increased, developed and controlled it would be possible to signal across space for considerable distances. My chief trouble was that the idea was so elementary, so simple in logic, that it seemed difficult to believe no one else had thought of putting it into practice. I argued, there must be more mature scientists who had followed the same line of thought and arrived at almost similar conclusions. From the first the idea was so real to me that I did not realize that to others the theory might appear quite fantastic."*
Guglielmo Marconi.

# Hertzian waves

Even when he was away, he carried his obsession with electricity with him. While he was with his mother, in the mountains of Biellese, in the Italian Alps of Lombardy, he was browsing through an electrical magazine. He came across an article written by his friend from Bologna, Professor Righi.

It was about the work of a German scientist named Heinrich Hertz who had died in January of that year. According to the article, Hertz had proved, seven years before, that there were electrical waves that *radiated through space* from one place to another. They *vibrated* through the air.

# The family of waves

It was not a new idea when Hertz proved it. In fact he had set out to test a prediction made by the Scottish scientist, James Clerk-Maxwell. Clerk-Maxwell, using mathematics, had worked out that

*"... when Hertz announced the results of his investigations, several scientists started experimenting in the hope of finding some means of utilizing these electromagnetic waves.*

*"Marconi, who was not really a scientist at all but merely an enthusiastic amateur with no professional qualifications, soon far outstripped the professionals in his ideas on the subject."*
Norman Wymer, from "Guglielmo Marconi".

light and heat were different forms of the *combined
forces* of electricity and magnetism.

He also said that the same combined force –
called electromagnetism – existed in a different
form, as an invisible disturbance, a vibration, which
moved (like visible light and audible sound) in
waves. He called this new form an *electromagnetic
wave.*

He calculated mathematically that electromagnetic waves would move and behave very like
water or sound waves, but that they would travel
at the speed of light – three hundred thousand
kilometres per second. He also predicted that
electromagnetic waves would be able to pass
through solid matter, gases and liquids, and easily
through a vacuum – space from which all air has
been removed.

But James Clerk-Maxwell worked this out by
mathematical calculations – intriguing, thought-
provoking, believed by most scientists to be true
… but nevertheless unproven.

Twenty-five years later, and eight years after
Maxwell died, Heinrich Hertz devised the experiment in 1887 that proved what Clerk-Maxwell had
said. The electromagnetic waves existed.

It was in that same year, that young Guglielmo
Marconi had entered the Leghorn Technical Institute and begun his unconscious march toward those
same electromagnetic waves.

## The dream takes shape

The moment Guglielmo read of Hertz's work, a
single question took possession of his brain. Could
*these* electrical waves be made to telegraph *without
wires?* If they could pass through air, could Hertz's
experiment be developed so that the waves would
travel not just across a room, but across cities,
countries, continents … to soar across the oceans?

Could they be made to transmit signals from one
place to another – signals that could be received
and understood? On board a ship, for example,
beyond sight and reach of land?

The question would not let go. Alfonso saw his

younger brother growing dreamy, that long summer in the mountains. He watched him scribble odd diagrams on scraps of paper. He seemed to churn thoughts and possibilities, and inner visions....

## Deflated

Summer waned, and Annie and the boys went back to the Villa Grifone. The day of their return Guglielmo saddled his donkey and rode to Professor Righi's house. He had to tell *someone* of the ideas that burned his brain!

Righi was not impressed. The waves might be new to Guglielmo, he explained, but they were not new to men of science, like himself. Since Hertz's first experiment had been published in 1888, scientists in several countries had been studying the waves. They had developed better ways of creating and detecting them, and could now produce waves of different lengths – much shorter than the ones Hertz had made.

*All Marconi's early trials of wireless were made at his home in Villa Grifone above the village of Pontecchio in Italy. Obsessed with his experiments, young Marconi shut himself away in his attic "laboratory", only occasionally saddling his donkey to ride into the nearest town of Bologna for more scientific supplies, or to visit the university library.*

Gently, but firmly, Professor Righi pointed out that, for all his enthusiasm, Guglielmo was unlikely to do something that they had not yet done. He was particularly unlikely to make important advances in science when his grasp of the basics, shown by his exam results, was still so shaky!

But he told Guglielmo about his own research over several years with Hertzian waves. He had repeated all Hertz's experiments and improved the apparatus. And he had found that the Hertzian waves became much weaker in the upper air.

Perhaps, he speculated, if you could make the waves *longer*, they might travel. But it would need an enormous electrical force to create waves long enough. It was probably impossible to do it successfully ... there was no way known.

Guglielmo left, deflated. But he was not deflected from his idea. He turned his donkey for Bologna, and rode to the library. He must find out *everything* about these electromagnetic waves.

## The pioneers of electromagnetism

He soon learned that Hertz's proof of the electromagnetic waves was the culmination of vital

*Opposite and below: The pioneers developed their equipment as they went along and had very primitive means for detecting electrical effects – often no more than a spark or buzzer that could be seen or heard. Today, sensitive equipment can track the smallest electrical and magnetic effect, undetectable to the human senses. Here, modern photography has achieved dramatic special effects.*

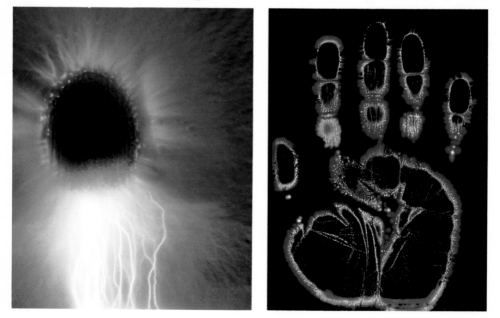

developments over the previous seventy years.

First had come proof of what had been long suspected: there was a definite connection between electricity and magnetism. It was in the winter of 1819-1820 that the Danish scientist, Hans Christian Oersted, showed this. He had simply revealed that if a wire carrying an electric current was held parallel and close to a magnetic needle, *but not touching it,* the electric current made the magnetic needle swing round.

He published his findings in the middle of 1820, and within weeks the trail was picked up by others. Over the next decades, scientists in France, the United States and Britain vastly extended understanding of this basic fact – so critical to all later developments: *electricity caused magnetism.* Now scientists had a versatile and powerful tool in their hands and lost no time in putting it to use.

Out of this knowledge, for example, came the electric needle-telegraph. They also discovered that, by coiling a wire in a certain way around a bar of soft iron and then passing electricity through the wire, you could turn the iron bar into a powerful magnet. Just as important, you could switch the

*The electromagnet – one of the earliest uses of electromagnetism: here, a large electromagnet is used to separate and lift heavy metal objects from waste material. When electricity is passed through the wire surrounding the iron core, it becomes a magnet that can hold very heavy objects firmly. As soon as the electricity is switched off, the object will fall.*

magnetism off again, simply by stopping the flow of electricity. They could bring a considerable power into existence, suddenly and at will, and just as suddenly destroy it!

This invention, known as an electromagnet, was at the heart of most inventions in those early years. Not least of these was the electric bell and the Morse telegraph: in both, a flow of electricity caused electromagnets to come into operation – to operate the hammers and ring the bell or to move the levers that tapped out the Morse code.

## Faraday

Then it was discovered that the reverse was also true: electricity produced magnetism, *magnetism produced electricity.* Just as you could turn an iron bar into a magnet by passing electricity close by, so you could create a flow of electricity in a wire by moving a magnet to and fro close to it.

This was the English scientist, Michael Faraday's, great discovery in 1831. He forged a vital link in understanding. It led, among other things, to the development of apparatus that could boost the electrical force scientists could generate. Now they could harness the *combined forces of magnetism and electricity,* using each to create and boost the other.

It culminated in Faraday's ideas that electricity and magnetism were not merely linked, but were different aspects of the *same phenomena:* that many of the known phenomena of the natural world – light and heat for example, were different forms of this phenomena, *electromagnetism.* For this all-embracing idea Faraday is known as the father of electromagnetism. It launched scientists onward to new applications for electricity at increasing speed as the century progressed, their ability to *use* electromagnetism often racing ahead of their understanding of what exactly was happening, and why. Even today, magnetism is not fully understood.

It was Faraday's ideas that James Clerk-Maxwell set out to investigate mathematically in 1873. It led him to predict that there were electric waves, invisible to the eye and as yet undetected, that were identical in nature to light, and just a different form of electromagnetism.

Hertz set out to prove they existed, and the waves he detected – which we now understand were radio waves – have gone down in history as Hertzian waves.

## Hertz's experiment

In the library, Guglielmo dug out Hertz's own published description of his work. What Hertz had done was to look for ways of making electricity spark into the air, and then see if he could detect it some distance away.

Hertz knew, from others' research, that if you shot a spark across a gap between two pieces of metal in a certain way, the electricity surged to and fro across the gap. It happened so fast that you couldn't see it – about five hundred million times a second. But he hoped that by creating a spark like this – a spark that *oscillated* – it would cause strong enough vibrations in the air for him to detect them. And he hoped to show that these vibrations were Clerk-Maxwell's electromagnetic waves.

So Hertz had organized his experiment: something to create the spark, and something to detect any disturbance in the air.

On one side he arranged a Leyden jar, which he linked to wires, connected in turn to two large brass plates. He left a small gap between the brass plates.

When he discharged electricity from the Leyden jar along the wires and across the gap between the brass plates, he succeeded in making an *oscillatory electrical spark* about five centimetres long jump the gap. All this was to be his "transmitter".

A few metres away, he put a circle of copper wire, with a small gap left in it. This made a much smaller "spark gap" – his "detector", or "receiver".

Then he shot electricity through his transmitter. As the big spark jumped across the gap between the brass plates of the transmitter, a tiny spark, a fraction of a millimetre long, jumped across the smaller gap in the copper wire circle.

He now had no doubt that some of the electricity passing through the transmitter gap had been radiated as an invisible wave across several metres of the room, reached the copper-circle receiver, and sparked across its gap.

Hertz set out to prove whether this unseen force behaved the way Clerk-Maxwell predicted. Did it move in waves? Could it be reflected, or bounced off things? One by one, he confirmed Clerk-Maxwell had been brilliantly right.

## Guglielmo grows bolder

The more Guglielmo read, the more convinced he was that his own ideas were right and Professor Righi's doubts not justified. Why should it not be possible to send these waves much, much further? There must be a way – pump more energy into the waves, make them larger, or find ways to detect them at greater distances.... Some instinct, much determination pushed him on, perhaps a hope that here was something he could do to make something of his life.

*A battery of Leyden jars as used in the 1890s by Marconi and other scientists. The Leyden jar was simply a device for storing electricity – electricity could be led into the jar along metal wires and chains, and held inside (for it would not pass through the glass easily), until it was later led out again or "discharged".*

He would try out Hertz's experiment himself. But he would need his mother's help. Urgently he explained that he needed a laboratory, somewhere to try out his ideas.

On the top floor of the Villa Grifone were two large, little-used rooms, linked by an open archway. They were known as "the attic". Nothing but trays of silkworms were stored there. Annie let him clear a little space among the trays. Busily Guglielmo assembled what he needed. The "attic" became his kingdom.

## The experiments begin

First, a battery, to provide the supply of electricity. Then something to boost the electrical force – an induction coil. This was one of the supreme inventions emerging from Faraday's work – so simple, so versatile and powerful. A soft iron bar, with wire wound tightly around it – a form of electromagnet.

But then over the top of this was wound a second wire. When a current of electricity from a battery was made to start and stop in the first wire – the

*The top floor of Villa Grifone, known as "the attic". Here, at the age of twenty, Marconi gathered his equipment, cleared some space on the silkworm benches, and began the experiments that would ultimately give practical radio to the world.*

"primary" as it was called – it caused or "induced" a much greater electrical force in the second wire – the "secondary". This force could be harnessed by linking it to other apparatus.

Copper wire, sheets of zinc and copper, tubes of metal filings ... one by one Guglielmo gathered his tools. It was going to be the same experiment that Hertz had done, but Guglielmo would try some changes. Professor Righi had told him about his own work, and loaned him some apparatus.

For example, Righi had improved Hertz's transmitter – he'd changed the "transmitter" spark gap slightly and the waves now went further. He'd put a curved piece of metal behind it, to reflect the waves toward the "receiver".

Nor did Guglielmo use Hertz's circle of copper wire with its small spark gap as his receiver. Scientists studying the Hertzian waves over the last few years had already found a much better way of detecting them.

## The Branly coherer

It was the result of several people's efforts. One had found that zinc and silver filings clung together when electricity was passed into them. Clinging together (cohering) like this, they allowed electricity to pass easily across them – that is, they became a good conductor.

In 1890, a French professor of physics, Edouard Branly, used this by making a glass tube filled with metal filings that could be connected at both ends to wires. This meant that a current of electricity could be sent through it easily.

His device was known as a coherer, because the metal particles "cohered" or clung together. The scientist Oliver Lodge in Britain – one of the main researchers into Hertzian waves – used the coherer successfully to detect them. It worked much better than Hertz's copper circle.

What happened was this: when electricity passed through a transmitter, the electromagnetic waves radiated across space and reached the coherer. The metal filings inside cohered.

*Above: A replica of Marconi's oscillator or spark gap, showing the spark passing between the metal balls.*

*Right: An oscillatory discharge of electricity between two metal objects. Heinrich Hertz knew that if you shot a spark across a gap between two pieces of metal in a certain way, the electricity surged to and fro across the gap about five hundred million times a second. It was this kind of spark that he, and later Marconi, used to create the electromagnetic waves.*

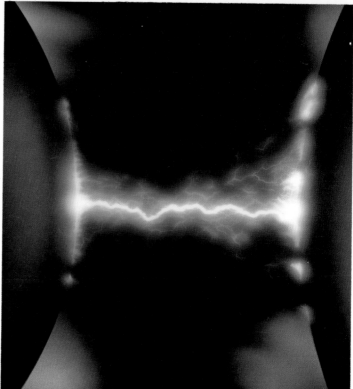

Now, because electricity passed easily across it, it formed a kind of switch: that is, it formed the necessary final link in a battery *circuit* – the continuous path for the electrical current to run along through the battery. The battery began operating, and could work a buzzer or bell.

Guglielmo put it all together; battery linked to induction coil and spark gap. A few metres away, coherer, battery and bell.

## The bell tinkles

If he had done it correctly, what should happen was this: he pressed a telegraphist's key to send a current of electricity through the battery and the induction coil, shooting along the wire, and across the gap between the metal balls with a great oscillatory spark. The electrical vibrations from this should travel out in all directions, in waves. Some should reach the coherer a few metres away.

With luck, good judgment and a sound grasp of all this, he should have arranged it so that the coherer would cohere, the battery switch on, and the bell ring.

He pressed the key. Instantly, the bell tinkled!

Excited, he checked the arrangement. Again he tapped the key. Again the bell tinkled! Again and again, he did it – just to make sure it always happened.

Greatly encouraged, he pressed on. Now to the first task: move the receiver further away, and see if he could get the electromagnetic waves to reach it.

## Struggle

He couldn't. He arranged the apparatus differently. He tried different wires – thicker, thinner, longer, shorter – searching for the best conductor of electricity.

He moved the metal balls to and fro, to make different size spark gaps. Air is a bad conductor of electricity, so the spark gap couldn't be too long or too short, or he wouldn't be able to create the kind of oscillatory spark needed to start the vibrations

> *"Marconi's staff gradually increased to some seven hundred, and he himself, instead of relying upon the help of just a few assistants, became the principal member of a highly specialized team. But though he was now less dependent upon his own inventive genius, he still worked just as energetically."*
> Norman Wymer, from "Guglielmo Marconi".

in the air. He fiddled with the induction coil, trying to increase the force of the electricity he shot through the transmitter.

There was little result. Days turned into weeks. He worked all day, then all night. His mother gave up trying to get him out of the attic for meals and took him a tray.

## Across the attic

He decided to try changing the transmitter a little. He connected metal plates to the balls of the spark gap. He did the same to each end of the coherer. Suddenly, the signals were so strong and clear, that he could send them from one end of the attic room to the other.

Thirty years later his mother told her granddaughter, Degna, of the night this happened. Near midnight, Annie was woken suddenly. Guglielmo, seething with suppressed excitement, was shaking her arm. He led her urgently up the stairs to his domain. There he stationed her to one side, among the clutter of silkworm trays. She watched him go to a telegraphist's key on a workbench under a window. He signed for her to listen.

Then he tapped the key with one finger. At the far end of the attic, instantly, a bell rang.

She did not fully understand the significance of what he had done, and it seemed a small mountain to have climbed for so many months of effort. But her son's excitement took hold of her. She redoubled her help, working to keep the peace of the household and leave Guglielmo to his experiments. She tried to still the grumblings of his father. Everything about his son's secretive hours in the attic worried Giuseppe. More time frittered away!

## The first leap

Meanwhile Guglielmo struggled to achieve greater distance. He tried everything he could think of. Then he tried it again, in different combinations. When something worked, he added it to his apparatus and moved on to some other improvement:

different materials for the balls of the spark gap; different metals for the coherer filings. Various ways of reducing them to dust. Hours went by, trial after trial, experiment after experiment.

The best mixture for the coherer seemed to be 95% nickel, 5% silver, ground to fine dust. He also changed the coherer: he narrowed the slit in which the dust rested; he altered the shape of the metal pieces inside each end of the glass tube, where wires could be connected. Then he found a way to pump air out of the tube and seal it, because he knew that electricity passed more easily through a vacuum than through air.

To his delight, the improvement was immense. Now the coherer detected the *slightest* amount of electricity reaching it, even very weak signals being sent from much further away.

## Try and try again

It wasn't that he had any particular idea that one thing would be better than another. He just tried them all, patiently, observing and recording the effects, using the ones that worked, discarding the ones that didn't. He got better at it: his hands more precise at manipulating the equipment, no matter how tiny. As his successes began to mount, his ideas became more confident.

Long winter months were passing. Dark, cold days; darker, colder nights, surrounded by batteries and coils and spark gaps among the silkworm trays.

Spring of 1895 came and went, and then the summer. Sometimes he saddled his donkey and went into Bologna for supplies. Most of the time he was in the attic.

He went on, tidying up, changing, developing his equipment. He must succeed in receiving signals at greater and greater distances.

Father loomed disapprovingly in the background. Mother, ever energetic and resourceful, tried to keep him away. Guglielmo was working on the coherer again. Once the filings had clung together you always had to tap them apart so they were ready to detect the wave from the transmitter.

It was frustrating having to cross the room and do this by hand. No usable system could have something so crude in it! He *must* make it happen automatically.

Once again the remarkable invention of the electromagnet came to hand. He included one in the apparatus of the receiver. Now every time the electrical current passed through the coherer, it attracted a little bar of soft iron with a minute hammer attached. Tap with the hammer on the coherer tube, and the filings were loose again!

He called this improvement a *decoherer.* A small change it might seem, but it was very important. Now each electrical impulse could be received and the apparatus immediately restored to readiness for the next one. It meant, therefore, that he could send impulses, each separate, clearly defined, in quick succession, that would be detected accurately by the coherer. It meant, therefore, that he could send and receive signals in *Morse code.*

The young man's vision soared again as he realized what he had done. Not simply waves sent and detected, but *intelligible signals.* Truly the

*Villa Grifone, Marconi's home. The attic "laboratory" was the top floor room on the right, marked by the plaque. From this window, Marconi tapped the signals that his brother Alfonso detected in various parts of the estate grounds, waving a white flag to show he had successfully received them.*

beginnings of a communication system!

The successes began to gather pace.

## Out of the attic

Until now the furthest he had sent a signal was from one end of the attic to the other. Now he moved beyond. He carried the receiver down to the floor below. His brother Alfonso stood guard to report if anything happened. Guglielmo hurried back to the attic. He pressed the Morse key. On the floor below, the bell sounded!

He moved the receiver to the next floor down....

Summer became harvest. There came the day when Guglielmo's receiver left the house and sat among the tubs of lemon trees on the terrace. Now the mysterious goings-on in the attic could be watched by family and estate workers alike. It became the focus of life on the farm.

Reluctantly, his father took an interest. He was yet unconvinced that this was different from his son's usual antics. Then Guglielmo gave a demonstration. Giuseppe expected to hear an unimpressive crackling from the receiver. Instead he heard the unmistakable three dots of the letter S in Morse code. Not just noises, but recognizable signals! Now the son's vision penetrated the father's mind: intelligible signals – transmitted across space!

He gave Guglielmo a little money to buy materials. He lectured him on doing his work carefully, so he could convince other men of its worth.

## The birth of wireless

By this time Marconi had achieved the same kind of distance, reliability and strength of signals as other experimenters had achieved in their laboratories and lecture rooms. But there was one major difference between them. Other scientists were exploring the general nature of the waves, how they worked, how they behaved if reflected or bounced off different substances. They aimed to extend understanding that these waves, visible light and radiant heat, were all part of one family of electromagnetic waves. Even today, scientists are

*"Guglielmo's father treated his son's request for money as he would have treated the request of any businessman. First, he had the boy explain the principles of his invention. His wife, fearful of a hitch, interceded with a plea that he be allowed to proceed on faith. Giuseppe rejected this approach out of hand on the grounds that if Guglielmo had, indeed, opened up a new scientific field he would need to know how to get really substantial financing and he would have to get it from men who did not invest 'on faith'. This was dampening but also encouraging. Giuseppe had tacitly admitted that Guglielmo might have a future and that it might involve big business."*

Degna Marconi, from her book, "My Father, Marconi".

still finding out more about how these waves move, and there is still much that is unknown.

In those early years it was vital research, combining in the years to come with Marconi's work, explaining it and shooting theoretical understanding of wireless forward to new heights.

Marconi, on the other hand, wasn't concerned with the theory. He was a practical man and had a single focus: make the waves travel *further:* use them to *send signals.* Everything was directed to this, and to this single-minded vision we owe the birth of practical wireless – of radio.

Guglielmo could not understand why someone had not already done what he planned to do. It was such a simple idea! It was just a case of finding out how.

It was the end of September 1895. Guglielmo Marconi was now twenty-one, and a year had passed since he had read of Hertz's work. He embarked on a new phase of experiment: boost the power of the transmitter: make longer waves or make the vibrations travel further ...

By now his transmitter had four balls – the two that formed the spark gap, each connected by a copper rod to two others. he took these outer two off, and instead fixed on two slabs of sheet iron from an old tank. He fixed similar slabs to the receiver.

Suddenly the waves went hundreds of metres!

## The giant leap

Then the breakthrough happened. As he sent his signals, he arranged and rearranged the equipment, ever searching for new solutions to old problems. By chance, he held one metal slab high above the ground, while the other rested on the earth.

Suddenly the signals were so strong that he could transmit them a kilometre away.

This was the furthest ever! He had not increased the energy being put into the spark. Yet suddenly the waves went further, simply because of a piece of metal in the air and a piece of metal on the ground.

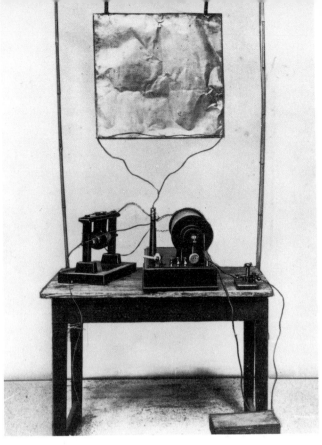

## Leaps and bounds

From now on progress was very fast: he tried the raised plate – the *aerial* – at greater and greater heights. He tried the other plate – the *earth* – buried in the ground. Instead of sheet iron he tried copper wire stretched into the air for the aerial, and a piece of copper buried in the ground for the earth. These he linked to the transmitter in the attic with a copper wire. He tried watering the ditch. He tried laying the plate horizontally in the ditch, then vertically. He tried it connected to other types of metal, then unconnected again. He added a similar aerial and earth on the receiver.

And now the receiver embarked on longer and longer journeys each day. It moved, carried in the arms of Alfonso, from field to field, vineyard to vineyard. The aerial, in the arms of an estate worker, brought up the rear of the cavalcade.

*The view from Marconi's attic window in Villa Grifone. It was over this steep hill that he realized he had successfully transmitted signals, proving to himself that radio waves continued to flow despite apparent geographical obstacles.*

## The other side of the hill

Marconi's signals were now transmitted over a kilometre and a half. He discovered that, while he sent them busily to Alfonso in one place, the waves were affecting another receiver he had placed on the *other side of the hill.*

Half disbelieving it had happened, half always knowing that it would, he prepared to repeat it. Alfonso was despatched with a hunting rifle, for his usual pole, topped with a white flag, would not be seen beyond the hill. From the attic Guglielmo watched his brother set off through the vineyards of ripening grapes, a farmer helping with the receiver and a carpenter carrying the aerial.

He saw them stride to the ridge of the hill, over the crest, and out of sight.

He waited a few minutes for them to settle in position. Then he tapped the Morse key. Far down the valley, out of sight, the shot echoed victoriously from Alfonso's rifle.

# To Britain

It was time for a family conference. Guglielmo could go no further with apparatus conjured from odds and ends among the silkworm trays: he needed far greater resources than could be gathered by the family alone.

They wrote first to the telegraph authorities in Italy. To their disappointment, the Italian Post Office was not interested in Guglielmo's invention. The Marconis turned instead to the other half of their family. Perhaps among Annie's relatives in England they would find someone to help.

By February of the next year, 1896, Annie and twenty-one-year-old Guglielmo were in London. They were more than lucky. One of Annie's nephews, Henry Jameson-Davis, took an immediate interest in his foreign relatives.

Henry was a thirty-year-old engineer. He had many contacts among scientists and business people in Britain, and from his first sight of Guglielmo's invention became greatly committed to his young cousin's efforts. He was in an ideal position to help: one of his scientist friends wrote a letter of introduction to William Preece, Chief Engineer to the British Post Office. So it happened that Guglielmo was directed straight to the one man in Britain most likely to be interested.

*"Marconi, who had no experience of business methods, wisely left the administrative side for others to attend to while he devoted his own energies to research. He worked extremely hard in his laboratory, and sometimes, when he had a particularly difficult problem to solve, would go two or three nights without sleep rather than stop before he had found the solution."*

Norman Wymer, from "Guglielmo Marconi".

# William Preece

Preece, then sixty years old, had been one of the very first telegraph engineers. Twelve years before he had begun investigating wireless communication created by "inducing" a current of electricity from one wire to another, without any wire connection between them. He had sent signals across water – by 1892 over four kilometres across the Bristol Channel. He had also used his induction system in Scotland between the mainland and the island of Mull when the submarine telegraph cable broke. But Preece also knew well that an induction system was limited over greater distances, and relied on long wires lying parallel to each other on each side of the water.

41

Taking as much of his apparatus as he could carry, Guglielmo set off to show Preece. Preece was instantly impressed. What possibilities for communicating between ships at sea, or between sea and land! He had long nursed the ambition to save ships from wreckage on the coast of Britain.

He arranged for more tests in his laboratories.

## First public demonstrations

Then came the first demonstrations for others. Guglielmo assembled his equipment on the roof of the General Post Office in London. It was July 27, 1896, a day recorded in history as the first public trial of practical wireless.

When all was ready, Guglielmo pressed his Morse lever. Away on the roof of another building about a kilometre off, the messages tapped gaily off on the Morse printing machine for all to see!

Events now moved faster than Guglielmo had ever dreamed. By September 2, the second demonstration for more Post Office representatives was ready, their ranks swelled by others from the British Army and Navy. Guglielmo's signals winged their way nearly three kilometres across the expanses of Salisbury Plain.

More adjustments to the equipment. More experiments with aerials: contraptions of wires and cylinders slung on tall poles; long wires held up by kites; metal plates reflecting the signals one way or another; aerials at different heights, angles, positions.... It kept them busy all through the winter and into the spring of the next year.

By March 1897, they sent signals up to seven kilometres; by May a record distance – nearly fourteen and a half kilometres between the mainland and Flatholm island in the Bristol Channel.

## A household name

From the moment of Marconi's successes on Salisbury Plain, newspapers in Britain and abroad swooped on the story. Journalists were intrigued by these goings-on in the air waves above the earth;

people thronged to hear public lectures about wireless. The young inventor fast became a household name.

July of 1897 brought particular happiness. Italy had realized its mistake in turning Guglielmo Marconi and his invention away and the government invited him to do tests for the Italian navy. The twenty-three-year-old inventor, failed entrant to the Italian navy, returned triumphantly to Italy and had the pleasure of sending the first ever ship-to-shore wireless signal.

These tests answered many other questions as well: what happened to signals when a ship changed position at sea? Or when land – islands or peninsulas – came between transmitter and receiver? And – most exciting for Guglielmo Marconi, for his inner eye never left his dream of world-wide communication – they could still send and receive signals when the ship was below the horizon. The curve of the earth – at least at these distances – did not stop wireless signals flowing.

*Marconi's first demonstration of his wireless to the Italian navy in 1897. In all his work in Italy, throughout the rest of his life, Marconi's untiring supporter and co-worker was his old boyhood friend, Luigi Solari.*

# Wireless stations

1897 was the year Marconi's company was founded, to become in his own lifetime a world-wide producer of communications systems. But in that first year of 1897, the new company's preoccupation was to make permanent wireless stations around Britain. Marconi and his team found hotel rooms, well-sited on the coast; there they installed transmitting and receiving apparatus and simple laboratory and workshop facilities.

The public flocked to watch, fascinated by the great masts in the hotel grounds hoisting aerial wires over thirty metres high. Most intriguing of all was the loud crash and crackle of the sparks that created the long wireless waves.

It was a time of frenetic activity. Guglielmo had scientists and mechanics working with him, each with their special skills. Yet still, as in the old days of Villa Grifone, they used any materials they could find so that the signals would keep flowing during an experiment. Grinding metal for coherers, heating wax for insulation, winding induction coils, adjusting spark gaps, fastening aerial wires, testing in small boats tossed in sea-gales – the demands on their stamina and ingenuity were endless. Guglielmo never tired, catching them all in his dream that one day, out of these small beginnings, would come world-wide wireless.

# From land to sea

The distances crossed grew longer. By the end of the year, new tests produced a reliable range of over forty-eight kilometres. They set up a new wireless link between a lighthouse on the mainland near Dover and the East Goodwins lightship nineteen kilometres out at sea. They were getting closer to Preece and Guglielmo's shared hope that wireless would save lives at sea.

Their hopes were fulfilled. Even as they worked, a ship drove aground on the Goodwin Sands and another collided with the lightship. Seasoned men of the sea were resigned to the grim death toll usually brought by accidents like these. But this

time was different: there was Marconi's wireless to summon lifeboats immediately to save the lives.

## The busy year

They were into the new year of 1898 – only two years since Guglielmo had arrived in England. It was a year of more success: the first ship-reporting service gave instant news of ships and cargos. And then came the world's first wireless sports report.

Summer yachting regattas around Britain's coast were popular events, particularly the Kingstown yacht races. People flocked in carnival mood to seaside towns to watch the large yachts sailing by. An Irish newspaper, the *Dublin Daily Express*, planned an exotic publicity scheme – minute-by-minute reports sent by Guglielmo's wireless from a tug behind the yachts to a shore station, and telephoned on to the newspaper office.

*Wireless captured the popular imagination, as shown by these cigarette cards of the 1900s picturing portable Marconi wireless stations. The tall structures on top are the aerials. People also flocked to lectures, demonstrations and exhibitions, eager to learn about the new invention.*

It was a great success, and a perfect test for the equipment. Even when the yachts were lost from view in rainy mists, the wireless kept working. Even drenched by waves, it never faltered.

## Across the English Channel

On March 27, 1899 wireless crossed the Channel between France and England – the first link between one country and another. It was only five years since the birth of Guglielmo's dream, and already wireless was leaping international boundaries. Congratulatory messages flashed to and fro, not least Guglielmo's thanks to Professor Branly for inventing the coherer.

The tests went on and on, throughout spring and early summer: between shore and moving warship; in storms; from a ship *simultaneously* with three stations. *The Times* newspaper reported this on April 24, 1899 with some emphasis. It was important, for it answered a major question about wireless: could you signal to one station without other signals cutting across and making your signals incomprehensible? Guglielmo had somehow made his receiver cut out an unwanted second signal. He was clearly on the track of the answer.

## To New York

The Kingstown races created interest in Marconi's wireless in the United States. A New York paper wanted to report the America's Cup yacht races in October 1899 in the same way. The United States navy, intrigued by Guglielmo's experiments for the British navy, was anxious to see his system.

So, in 1899 twenty-five-year-old Guglielmo went to the United States, reported the races and did tests for the navy. These did more than show the range and reliability of his system – it gave further proof of its life-saving gift to the world. During testing, someone fell overboard from a battleship and would almost certainly have drowned. But an emergency wireless message from the battleship reached a cruiser steaming behind, and she instantly

*Opposite: Marconi in 1903. It was only eight years since he had conceived his revolutionary apparatus on the silkworm benches at Villa Grifone. By 1903, at the age of twenty-nine, Marconi was world-famous for his scientific breakthrough, heading a large company that designed and made wireless equipment, and employing some of the most skilled and imaginative scientists and technical experts of the age.*

launched a boat to the rescue.

Guglielmo's key worry remained, however. He had not fully solved the problem of interference from signals between different receivers and transmitters. He must make it possible to accept signals at *one chosen wavelength,* and ignore all others. Only then could two ships, their transmitters and receivers tuned to the same wavelength, exchange messages freely, while others continued with messages at different wavelengths.

Guglielmo returned to Britain preoccupied with the problem. Ahead lay the year he would solve it, and the year he would begin his march to his greatest triumph – wireless across the Atlantic.

## The great challenge

The Atlantic was an enormous challenge. Many scientists believed that electromagnetic waves could not follow the curve of the earth, but moved in straight lines, like a light beam. The bulge of the Atlantic (because of the earth's curve) was over two hundred and forty kilometres high between the United States and Britain. Surely it would send the

*The Marconi permanent transatlantic station at Glace Bay, Cape Breton, Nova Scotia. All the transatlantic stations needed huge aerial systems to catch the minutest amount of electrical energy spreading out from a transmitter thousands of kilometres away.*

waves off into space!

But Guglielmo had already transmitted to ships below the horizon – hidden from view by the *curve of the earth*. He was equally certain that the transatlantic link could be made. Increase the power, improve the receiver ... the solution would be found. He had already moved beyond the old metal dust coherer to new, more sensitive detectors. There would be other solutions, yet undreamed of. It *could* be done.

He began to plan for the transatlantic trials. First, he must find suitable sites for the stations – one in the United States, one in Britain.

By October of 1900 they found the British site: Poldhu on the coast of south-west Cornwall. It was the closest they could get to the continent of America over three thousand kilometres away. Early in the new year Guglielmo chose Cape Cod in Massachusetts for the American site. Between the Cape and Poldhu there was only water.

With his Chief Engineer, Vyvyan, who had supervised the building at Poldhu, he went to Cape Cod. Vyvyan began arrangements to build the station.

## Disaster strikes

By September 1901 the new, specially-designed equipment was installed at Poldhu – a vastly more powerful transmitter and a great ring of masts. It rose sixty-one metres high on the cliffs, in a circle sixty-one metres across. At Cape Cod in the United States, the sister station was nearly ready.

Then disaster struck. On September 15, a gale roared across Poldhu and left the giant ring of masts and aerials a tangled mess across the cliff.

Determined activity cleared the wreckage in a week, and they began tests with simpler aerials.

In November, the Cape Cod aerial keeled over. Gone was Guglielmo's hope to exchange signals between two powerful stations.

But he would not accept it. He decided to abandon his plan to send as well as receive signals in the United States. Instead he would just try to receive them from Poldhu.

# Kites and balloons

Newfoundland off the east coast of Canada, facing across the Atlantic to Britain, seemed best. By the end of November, the team set sail: Marconi, George Kemp (who had worked with him since the first trial for Preece) and another assistant, Paget.

With balloons and kites to raise the aerial wire as high as possible, they landed at St. John's in Newfoundland on Friday, December 6, 1901. By Tuesday, they were ready for their first kite trial. First, a cable telegraph to Poldhu, arranging for them to send signals for a fixed period every afternoon. The signal would be the three dots of the Morse letter S.

But next day the weather was worse, with a high wind blowing. Kemp struggled to launch the vast balloon that carried the aerial, wrestling furiously with the guidelines. Inside the building, Guglielmo adjusted the equipment over and over again. Earphones crackled and hissed. He tried to pick out three dots from the wind's howl.

# Three dots across the Atlantic

He could detect nothing. He tried again. Still nothing. Then, in mid-afternoon, just as he caught a few weak dots, the wind ripped the balloon from its mooring and valiant Kemp.

Next day one kite was lost to the wind. They launched the second kite. It dived and soared, tearing frantically at its moorings, and with each swoop it changed the height of the aerial, changed its ability to receive signals.

But Guglielmo heard them – unmistakably – the three dots across the Atlantic. First one set, then another, and then an hour later, a third.

To go any further, however, they needed fixed aerials on high masts, as they had first planned.

They could not do this in Newfoundland. The local cable telegraph company resented Guglielmo's wireless experiments and took legal action to stop them. The team moved instead to Nova Scotia in Canada, where the government was willing to let

*Opposite: Marconi's exploits seized the imagination of many artists. Here is one version showing Marconi receiving the first transatlantic signal in Newfoundland in 1901. In fact, the team that achieved this, battling in icy blizzards with aerials on kites and balloons, consisted of just three men – Marconi and his two skilled assistants, Kemp and Paget.*

51

*Marconi's company was founded in July of his second year in Britain, 1897. Its purpose was to develop and sell his invention, and it rapidly became a world-wide supplier of radio equipment. Here workers assemble radio apparatus at the London factory in about 1906.*

them have land. There, at Glace Bay, on the peninsula of Cape Breton, they prepared for their new transatlantic station.

There was much journeying to and fro across the Atlantic as building the new site gathered pace. Guglielmo brought more experienced engineers and operators from Britain, including Vyvyan again.

On each of these sea voyages extensive tests with wireless amassed more information. For example, signals were much clearer by night than by day: night range could be three-times more than the day range. These were early clues to problems that would bedevil them throughout the next years – the erratic, unpredictable, uncontrollable results that would not be explained until the 1920s. It was only then that scientists would finally understand the *ionosphere.*

## The ionosphere

This is several layers of electrically-charged particles high up in the atmosphere. They result from the sun's radiation, and wireless waves bounce off them, bending back toward the earth's surface. *Here* was the reason that wireless waves did not shoot off into space; and here, too, the reason for the night-day difference – the different activity of the sun by day and by night. But it would be over twenty years from Guglielmo's first S across the Atlantic before scientists knew enough about the ionosphere to use it for manipulating wireless signals as they wished.

In 1901 and 1902 there were a thousand obstacles to be overcome. Not until December 1902 were the first readable signals sent across the Atlantic to Poldhu. Great relief at Glace Bay! But next time – failure. Erratic results continued to frustrate them, incomprehensible because no one knew about the ionosphere. Although the transatlantic service was now open, it was not really workable. Some messages had to be sent twenty-four times before they reached Britain. Then, the Glace Bay aerial fell down. All three transatlantic stations had lost their aerials.

It was an unhappy time for Marconi, thwarted by these unknown laws of nature. Getting it right occupied him month after month, year after year.

## Wireless develops world-wide

Wireless had come a long way from his work in the attic of Villa Grifone. Skilled people throughout the world were bringing a vast range of technical development – tighter control of wavelengths and much longer ranges for the same electrical power.

The way was open to wireless telephony – words sent as speech instead of Morse code. Once wireless could transmit the spoken word, it was only a short distance to broadcast entertainment – music and

*"The unprecedented job cut out for this young Italian was to conquer space, shrivel the size of a 25,000 mile sphere and weave his fellowmen closer together in an invisible web of lightening-like communication; to make an international whispering gallery of the heavens."*
Orrin P. Dunlap, from his biography, "Marconi: The Man and his Wireless".

*"Marconi was still only twenty-seven when he sent his first signal across the Atlantic; and he lived to the age of sixty-three. During the second half of his life he saw radio gradually develop – just as he had predicted – into a vast commercial undertaking, a world-wide network; and he even lived to see the first experiments with television."*
Norman Wymer, from "Guglielmo Marconi".

*An advertising sign for a Marconi supplier. By 1912, the Marconi Company was producing standard wireless equipment in large numbers, particularly for ships. It had also begun work on wireless communication for aircraft.*

plays on radio and television. And the invention of a new kind of detector, the thermionic valve, by Ambrose Fleming brought a burst of achievement in wireless technology in the next decades.

## Seventeen hundred lives saved

In 1909, a liner cruising the Atlantic collided with another ship. Devastated, and with ruptured electricity supplies, the stricken ships lurched helplessly in fog-bound waters. But the wireless on the liner remained intact.

A young wireless operator, Jack Binns, switched instantly to emergency batteries and sent the call for help. Forty-eight kilometres away on shore, the call was heard. Thick mists hid the foundering ships from rescuers, but wireless kept guiding them on.

What triumph when a liner finally found them and rescued nearly seventeen hundred people! The only deaths were the five killed on collision. Wireless operator Binns arrived to cheering crowds in New York and back home in Britain. Again, Marconi's name was linked throughout the world with saving lives at sea.

## The unsinkable Titanic

The power of Marconi's wireless was proved again, pitifully, in April of 1912. On the fifteenth, the largest, most luxurious, "unsinkable" ocean liner yet built sank to the bottom of an icy sea and fifteen hundred people died. The only survivors were those saved by wireless.

It was the *Titanic's* maiden voyage, to a fanfare of publicity: the most up-to-date technology, the richest, most famous passengers sporting the most glittering fashions....

At 11:40 p.m. on the night of Sunday, April 14, she struck an iceberg. Two hours forty minutes later, she disappeared beneath the frozen waters of the North Atlantic.

The *Carpathia* had heard the *Titanic's* wireless call for help. But she was sixty miles away. She arrived two hours after the black waters had swallowed the great liner and rescued over seven

*Throughout the first decades of the twentieth century, Marconi's name was linked again and again with saving lives at sea, for only his wireless enabled a ship in distress to summon help immediately. The lives lost when the "Titanic" sank proved pitifully clearly how effective radio communication could be – if only people used it properly.*

hundred survivors. About fifteen hundred people had died: there weren't enough lifeboats for them.

Wireless ice warnings had been ignored. Most shocking of all to those who already knew the power of wireless, calls for help from the *Titanic* to a ship close enough to save everyone *before* the *Titanic* went down, were not heard. The exhausted wireless operator was off duty. The survivors owed their lives only to the *Carpathia's* operator. Already off duty, he had returned on a sudden, unexplained impulse, and heard the distress call.

The tragedy proved again what had been shown so clearly a year before when wireless had saved the seventeen hundred. It would bring many changes in safety measures at sea, not least the installation of wireless on most ships, with enough operators to work it continually round the clock.

1912 was also a year of personal disaster for Guglielmo. A road accident in Italy left him with a badly-injured right eye. The doctors believed this posed dangers for the other, good eye, and they removed the damaged one. It took him months to recover, but in the end he returned to work, occupied at first with improving the transatlantic service. But in 1916 he made a new, very significant decision. He had become increasingly curious about the possibilities of short wireless waves.

Now he decided to investigate this further. He was in hospital at the time in Genoa with a septic throat, and typically he lost no time in getting to work. He asked for a special, small aerial with a square reflector to be designed and brought to him in the hospital. There in the long corridor, with his old friend Luigi Solari helping him, he started experiments with ultra short waves. But he realized fast that, just as with long waves years before, he needed extensive tests on short-wave wireless over long ranges.

## "Elettra"

He found his solution, and satisfied a life-time ambition. He bought a ship which he named *Elettra*. It was over sixty-one metres long, and with its crew of thirty, capable of sailing almost anywhere. Guglielmo cruised happily in it for the first time in the spring of 1920 – his floating laboratory for short-wave research, and from now on, his home. He filled the cabins with friends, family and famous visitors – among them the monarchs of Italy, Spain, and George V and Queen Mary of Britain. The glittering parties on *Elettra* were famous for the music broadcast direct from London. Entertainment broadcasting was just beginning.

## Short waves and long waves

Very different wireless systems arose out of different lengths of wireless wave. Long wave wireless had waves hundreds of metres long: it needed enormous aerials – vast masts with long wires pointing in the direction of transmission, and stations like those at Poldhu and Glace Bay with power to send signals thousands of kilometres.

Short waves were only tens of metres long: short-wave aerials could be much smaller and more tightly

focused in one direction, like a beam: you could communicate over long distances with only a fraction of the power needed by long-wave systems. Ultra short waves, by contrast, were measured in metres, and needed even smaller aerials.

Throughout both 1922 and 1923 Guglielmo concentrated on short-wave wireless. His company prepared for a new Imperial Wireless Scheme using short-wave beam stations all over the British Empire. Within four years, by October 1926, they had achieved it. Short-wave beam stations began working in South Africa, India, Australia, the United States and South America.

*After World War I, Marconi began to undertake many diplomatic and political duties for Italy, acting as an ambassador for his country. He was Italy's delegate to the Paris Peace Conference that followed the war.*

## Marconi's dream comes true

It was the realization of Guglielmo's dream, that vision of world communications he had at the Villa Grifone thirty-two years before. Now the fifty-two-year-old Marconi began to move back from the preoccupations that had driven him since he was twenty.

In his final years, he turned again to the country

Modern uses of radio range far and wide.

Above: Communications satellites receive radio signals from one point on earth, and return them to another place on earth – making possible long-distance radio telephony and instant television broadcasting across the globe.

Above right: Radio (with a special aerial) is even used to detect the thickness of ice in the Antarctic.

Right: A portable transistor radio powered by battery offers entertainment to listeners in a village market in Nigeria – far from any permanent electricity supply.

of his birth, living mainly in Italy.

Over the next years a succession of heart attacks taxed Marconi's energies, and he was able to return to research fully only in the 1930s. In the last years he was interested in wireless waves of very short length – microwaves less than a metre long.

## The Marconi legacy

Guglielmo Marconi was taken ill and died in the early hours of July 20, 1937. He was sixty-three years old. News of his death sped by wireless around the world. Stations everywhere closed down, remembering in their two minutes' silence, the world before Guglielmo's wireless began its unforgettable transformation.

It is impossible to imagine our world without communications that link continents in an instant. Wherever people need contact with others – in remote places or on the move – for safety or protection, rescue and help, for sharing information, then

*"The world must judge Marconi as a wireless man, because this was what he chose to be. All other roles were to him minor ones, taken up lightly because of circumstances, convention, or a lesser passion than that which drove him to create great communication systems."*
*William P. Jolly, from his book "Marconi".*

*A modern ship's radio
room. Radio has its most
obvious use – for security,
communications and
rescue services – whenever
people are on the move.
Even now, in the rooms of
the Villa Grifone, where
Marconi developed the
first working radio,
research continues to
perfect the use of radio
waves of very short length
– microwaves – for
radiophones across
international boundaries.*

wireless plays its irreplaceable role. Ambulances and fire-services, air, sea and land rescue, police and army in the modern world – all spring from the power of instant contact given by wireless – by radio. Ocean depths and outer space are within communicating range. And for us all there is the immediate entertainment of radio and television in our own homes.

We do not owe the discovery of the scientific principles to Guglielmo Marconi: but we owe him that vast first leap to a usable system. We have him to thank for the imagination, the single-minded vision of how to apply new scientific knowledge, and the immense speed with which he did it.

And we owe to Marconi alone that great gift of wireless for those in danger on the sea and in the air. There can be no more fitting legacy for the man who had two driving preoccupations in his life – to harness electromagnetic waves for human use and his unchanging love of the sea.

# Important Dates

| | |
|---|---|
| 1745 | The Leyden Jar is invented simultaneously in three places and named after the Dutch city of Leyden. |
| 1752 | Benjamin Franklin discovers that electricity is related to lightning. |
| 1800 | Alessandro Volta invents the electric battery. |
| 1819-20 | Hans Christian Oersted, a Danish scientist, discovers that electricity and magnetism are closely related – electricity causes magnetism. His work is swiftly developed by Ampère. |
| 1825 | In Britain, William Sturgeon discovers the electromagnet, which is developed in the United States by Joseph Henry. |
| 1831 | In Britain, Michael Faraday discovers that magnetism produces electricity. This leads to the harnessing of combined forces of electricity and magnetism as different aspects of the same phenomenon, electromagnetism. He invents the induction coil. |
| 1837 | In Britain, Charles Wheatstone and William Cooke introduce an electric needle telegraph, developed from Oersted's discovery. |
| 1843 | In the United States, Samuel Morse transmits the first message along a telegraph wire based on the electromagnet. |
| 1866 | The Atlantic telegraph is finally laid successfully. |
| 1873 | James Clerk-Maxwell investigates Faraday's ideas and predicts mathematically that there are electric waves, which exist as a form of invisible disturbance or vibration, and move at the speed of light. They are a form of electromagnetism. |
| 1874 | April 25: Guglielmo Marconi is born in Bologna, Italy. |
| 1876 | Alexander Graham Bell invents the telephone. |
| 1887 | Marconi fails to get into Leghorn Naval Academy. In the winter he goes to Leghorn Technical Institute to study physics and chemistry. Heinrich Hertz devises an experiment to prove that Clerk-Maxwell is correct. The electromagnetic waves are named Hertzian waves. |
| 1890 | A French scientist, Edouard Branly, invents the coherer which replaces Hertz's copper circle. |
| 1894 | Marconi begins his wireless experiments. |
| 1895 | Marconi invents his decoherer. He sends his first signal over the hill near Villa Grifone. |
| 1896 | Guglielmo, aged twenty-one, and his mother go to England after the Italian Post Office refuse to see his invention.<br>July 27: The first public trial of the practical wireless takes place in London.<br>Sept 2: Marconi signals three kilometres over Salisbury Plain, England. |
| 1897 | May: Marconi signals fourteen-and-a-half kilometres across the Bristol Channel.<br>July: Marconi sends the first ship-to-shore wireless signal during tests for the Italian navy.<br>Marconi's "Wireless Telegraph Company" is founded. |

| 1899 | Marconi sends a wireless signal across the English Channel. |
|------|---|
| 1900 | Marconi introduces important developments in tuning. |
| 1901 | Dec 13: The Morse Code "S" is sent from Poldhu, Britain and heard in Newfoundland, Canada. |
| 1904 | In Britain, J.A. Fleming invents the thermionic valve or "electron valve" – a very sensitive detector of radio waves, which makes possible the future development of radio-telephony and broadcasting. |
| 1905 | March 16: Thirty-year-old Guglielmo Marconi marries Beatrice O'Brien. Marconi introduces the horizontal directional aerial. This becomes very important in increasing the range of long-distance transmissions. |
| 1907 | In the United States, the Fleming thermionic valve is significantly developed by Lee de Forest. |
| 1909 | Wireless saves 1700 people from a shipwreck. Marconi is awarded the Nobel Prize for Physics jointly with Carl Ferdinand Braun of Germany. |
| 1912 | April 14/15: The "unsinkable" Titanic hits an iceberg on her maiden voyage. The survivors are saved by the wireless operator sending signals for help. Marconi loses an eye. |
| 1915 | During, and after, World War I Marconi undertakes many diplomatic missions for Italy. |
| 1919 | Marconi is Italian delegate to the Paris Peace Conference. |
| 1920s | Entertainment broadcasting begins. |
| 1926 | Several short-wave beam stations are in operation. |
| 1927 | June: Marconi marries for a second time, to Christina Bezzi-Scali. |
| 1937 | July 20: Guglielmo Marconi dies at the age of sixty-three. |

# Further reading

Catherall, Ed: *Electric Power,* Wayland, 1981.
Dunlap, Orrin E.: *Marconi the man and his wireless,* Macmillan (New York), 1937.
Jolly, W.P.: *Marconi,* Constable, 1972.
Kerrod, Robin: *Messages on the Move,* Grafton Books, 1986.
Marconi, Degna: *My Father Marconi,* Muller, 1962.
Stansell, John: *Discovering Communications,* Longman, 1983.

# Scientific Terms

**Aerial (Antenna):** That part of a *radio* system from which wireless or radio waves are transmitted into, or received from, space or the atmosphere.

**Battery:** A number of compartments or cells containing liquid chemicals, linked by different metals, arranged in a series or parallel to each other. These produce a continuous flow of electricity – an *electric current.*

**Coherer:** An early form of *detector* of wireless waves.

**Conductor:** A material through which electricity flows easily. Non-conductors – materials through which electricity will *not* pass easily – are used to insulate electrical wiring.

**Detectors:** Devices for detecting when a wireless wave had been received – for example, a *coherer* or a *valve,* or magnetic and crystal detectors.

**Electric current:** A continuous flow of electricity through a *conductor.*

**Electromagnet:** A temporary magnet formed by winding wire around a soft piece of iron. When an *electric current* flows through the wire, the iron becomes a magnet.

**Induction coil:** This has a soft-iron core with two windings of wire wrapped around it – the primary and the secondary. When an *electric current* is made to start and stop in the primary, a much greater electrical force is induced in the secondary.

**Morse code:** A code for converting letters into a pattern of dots and dashes. Used in the telegraph or wireless, the dots and dashes became long and short clicks or buzzer sounds. If a Morse writer was connected, it could make long and short marks on paper through an ink ribbon.

**Radio:** The use of electromagnetic waves to transmit or receive electrical signals without wires. In its widest sense it includes sound broadcasting, television and radar. To transmit by radio, a transmitter feeds a transmitting *aerial,* from which electromagnetic waves are sent out as ground or sky waves to a receiving *aerial* which feeds the *receiver.*

**Receiver:** The equipment for receiving radio waves. It consists of a device for detecting radio waves, and equipment for translating that into a form that can be heard or seen.

**Transmitter:** The equipment required to send out *radio* signals to the receiving part of the system.

**Tuning:** Making equipment accept signals at one particular *wavelength.*

**Vacuum:** A space in which there are relatively few gas molecules or atoms. For example, the space from which all air has been removed.

**Valve:** A later device than the *coherer* for detecting and amplifying *radio* waves.

**Wavelength:** Literally, the length of the wave. Long waves are hundreds of metres long. Short waves are tens of metres long. Ultra-short waves are metres long and microwaves are under a metre long. The associated idea of "frequency" means the frequency of a wave motion in a particular time period.

# Index

ROCK AROUND THE

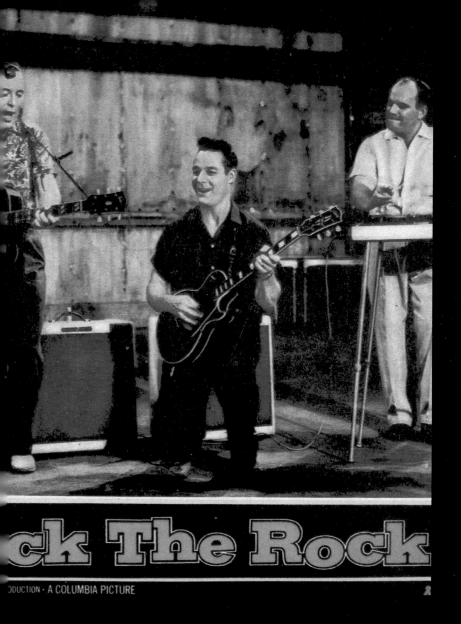

ck The Rock

ODUCTION · A COLUMBIA PICTURE

dca
RELEASE

THE KING OF
ROCK 'N' ROLL!
ALAN
FREED
IN

ROCK, ROCK, ROCK

# Don't Kno

A CLOVE

ck The Rock

DUCTION · A COLUMBIA PICTURE

# CONTENTS

# THE AGE OF ROCK

Alain Dister

DISCOVERIES

HARRY N. ABRAMS, INC., PUBLISHERS

The year was 1945. World War II had just ended in a flash over Hiroshima. The GIs came back home longing for peace and domestic happiness, but found that the old values were dying. And the music—young people were turning their backs on the old-fashioned sounds of the conservative white adult world, more attracted to the fresh and witty sound of certain black singers.

CHAPTER I
# THE PIONEERS

Black rhythm and blues seduced young white music lovers with its raw energy. Its heir, rock and roll, produced a similar passion, though the songs of Bill Haley (opposite), for example, could not claim the vitality of their models.

1954. General Dwight David Eisenhower was president. Ten years earlier his GIs had made history on the beaches of Normandy and all across Europe. Ever since, the United States had been considered the international symbol of rediscovered liberty and happiness.

Nevertheless, the Cold War was in full swing, stirred up by the seemingly permanent menace of nuclear conflict with the USSR. The fear of Communism incited a witch-hunt led by Senator Joseph McCarthy, and intellectuals were his first victims.

But this repressive atmosphere did not impede the strong artistic current flowing between New York and San Francisco. It was the time of beatniks, of (to use the Beat terms) desolation angels and celestial bums, rebels, and lovers of jazz, poetry, and the road. They even looked alike: writers Jack Kerouac and his friend Neal Cassady, actors James Dean and Marlon Brando, and artists Jackson Pollock and Robert Frank, with their T-shirts, blue jeans, and leather jackets, and their cool looks, guarded gazes, and provocative smiles—all fragile, crazy, and free.

In the mid-fifties James Dean (above left) and Marlon Brando (above) personified the rebellious teenager.

## America in Black and White

Behind Kerouac's literary road and the photographic path taken by Frank loomed a country that was a victim of its own emptiness and immobility, no longer looking forward to anything, without future, without hope. The pursuit of happiness guaranteed by the Constitution found its realization in a consumer frenzy and a petty regulated existence in which dangerous—or immoral—activities such as sexual relations, motorcycle rides, and certain types of dancing were prohibited. Middle-class white society

Neal Cassady (below left) was the model for the hero of *On the Road*, the novel-manifesto of the Beat Generation written by his friend Jack Kerouac (below right).

prospered, resigned, self-satisfied, and suspicious of its neighbors—particularly its black neighbors.

One hundred years after the end of the Civil War, blacks did not enjoy their full civil rights. Southern states still practiced segregation, and most blacks' economic level, urban as well as rural, was extremely low. Set apart culturally from the white community, blacks invented their own forms of expression, particularly in the musical field, and created systems of independent distribution for it: record labels, concert circuits, local radio stations. Simply by listening to those stations, white teenagers discovered, to their great relief, music far more lively than the standards being sung by Bing Crosby and Frank Sinatra, the stars of the day.

## Blacks Invented a New Dance, Rock and Roll

Everything began with, on the one hand, jazz and blues —especially boogie-woogie—and, on the other, gospel. The first kind of music was played in the bars, "juke joints," and dance halls; the second was sung in churches. In fact, some of the biggest rock and rhythm and blues artists made their debuts accompanied by small, out-of-tune organs, behind a preacher. Vocal groups like the Ink Spots, which were very popular in the thirties, were also descended from gospel. One music would devote itself to the secular virtues of teenage romance, and the other would remain deeply religious.

Blues singers occasionally found more lucrative outlets in bands that played on the weekends for social occasions. One popular dance, developed in the forties, was named "rock and roll." To balance, to roll, to reel, to spin…the graphic vocabulary of the black world had little in common with repressed white ways when it came to describing physical or sexual pleasure. Often backed by a honking saxophone, certain singers known as "shouters" had begun to emphasize the beat by screaming, a technique inherited directly from preachers. Little Richard, Screamin' Jay Hawkins, and, to a lesser extent, Ray Charles, exemplify this style.

A pianist, organist, saxophonist, and—primarily— a singer, much inspired by gospel music, Ray Charles

At the beginning of the fifties, teenagers were unhappy with the world being offered them and turned to popular black rhythms to help them reinvent a style, a music, an attitude. Right: Ray Charles, the great voice of gospel-flavored blues.

skillfully combined the best of blues, jazz, and soul. Discovered by Atlantic Records producer Jerry Wexler, Ray Charles recorded several tunes in the fifties that were immediately popular with young audiences: "I Got a Woman," "What'd I Say," and "Hit the Road, Jack." Strongly influenced by rhythm and blues, this

was rock and roll music
before the term was
even defined.

### Fats Domino

Enormously exciting for the
teenagers who discovered it, this
music was often recorded in makeshift studios in
Memphis, St. Louis, and Chicago, on the old migration
path to the North, marking these cities as
capitals of the blues. Black radio stations in
the South were the first to broadcast it, well
before big cities like New York or Los
Angeles. Small labels (Vee Jay, Ace, King)
flourished, featuring stars like Howlin' Wolf—
who recorded in Memphis with producer Sam
Phillips—Muddy Waters, and Sonny Boy Williamson.

The first bands of
pianist Fats Domino
(below) were already
playing rock and roll at
the end of the forties.

They were great musicians, experienced bluesmen who charged up the old blues idiom with electricity.

At the same time further south, in New Orleans, pianists ruled, playing a musical style born in the brothels and barrelhouses of the French Quarter. Dave Bartholomew ("The Monkey") and Fats Domino ("Blueberry Hill," "My Blue Heaven," "Ain't That a Shame") played a kind of music that combined the influences of boogie-woogie, traditional jazz inherited from Jelly Roll Morton and Fats Waller, and the energetic rhythm and blues of dance halls. They enjoyed a solid local reputation well before the historic appearance of rock and roll.

### The Exact Date of the Birth of Rock and Roll Is Difficult to Determine

Was rock and roll born in late 1951, when the irrepressible and melodramatic singer Johnnie Ray imitated dance-hall shouters? Or in July 1954, when a shy young man, Elvis Presley, is said to have knocked on the door of Sam Phillips' studio with the idea of cutting a record for his mother's birthday? Or in

The children of white puritan society derived a certain pleasure in singing lyrics with suggestive innuendos. "Shake," "rattle," "rock," and "roll" evoked, in a roundabout way, amorous passion and physical release. Black musicians commonly used such jubilant expressions. Their white imitators, like Bill Haley, toned down the meanings to shield themselves from censure and to increase record sales.

Johnnie Ray (below) invented a very personal style. In the course of his concerts, he cried, begged, choked, and went into contortions. Many early rockers modeled themselves on him.

March 1955, when the film *Blackboard Jungle* made Bill Haley's "Rock Around the Clock" a smash hit? Or, that same year, when disc jockey and promoter Alan Freed claimed to baptize the new fashionable dance with the name "rock 'n' roll"?

The date matters little: This music, in one form or another, had existed for a long time. What changed is that certain show-business tycoons calculated that if rock and roll remained exclusively black property, blacks would receive all the profits—and the profits would necessarily be limited. It seemed critical to open rock up to the huge white market. But the moguls needed an acceptable product—what white teenager could identify with the potentially off-putting image of a Howlin' Wolf or a Sonny Boy Williamson? The new image of rock and roll would be one decked out with all the appropriate enticements of youth, beauty, and rebelliousness. James Dean in *Rebel Without a Cause* and Marlon Brando in *The Wild One*

**THE ELVIS PRES**

**STARRING**

**IN PERSON**  ★

# ELVIS

★

# PRESLEY

WITH AN **ALL STAR CAST**

**THE JORDONAIRES**

**PHIL MARAQUIN**

**FRANKIE CONNORS**

**BLUE MOON BOYS & Others**

# FLORIDA T

**JACKSONVILLE -**

# FRI · SAT AUG

**EY SHOW** had already shown the way. They embodied this vague feeling of defiance against an adult world perceived as a generator of boredom, submission, and cowardice.

### "If I Could Find a White Man Who Had the Negro Sound and the Negro Feel, I Could Make a Billion Dollars" —Sam Phillips

Elvis Presley grabbed the opportunity. A truck driver with slightly too-long hair, flashy clothing, and a crooked half-smile, he looked like a rebel: The exterior seemed hard, but the heart was tender. He loved his parents, his mother especially, and visited churches more often than bars. His only fault, in the eyes of staunch Southern traditionalists, would be his interest in black music.

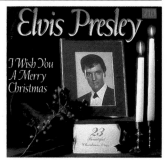

The devout Elvis practiced by singing hymns and accompanying himself on the organ at home.

Once he became famous Elvis was always accompanied by professional guitarists and held a guitar only when posing for the camera. Overleaf: Elvis in concert, 1956. Pages 24–5: From *Loving You*, 1957.

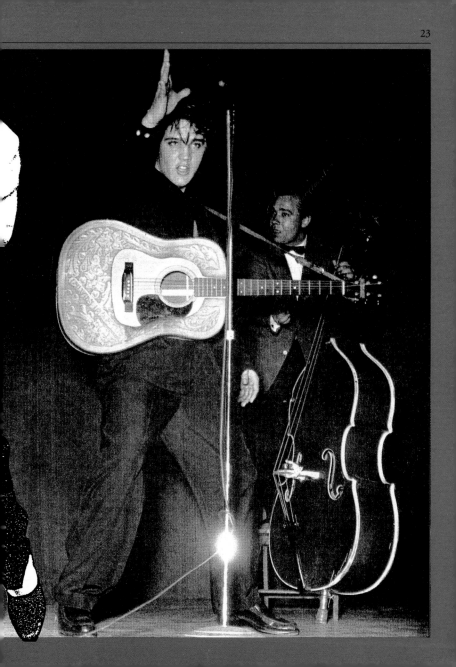

Presley, born in 1935 in Mississippi, was familiar with B. B. King, Howlin' Wolf, Arthur "Big Boy" Crudup, and all the other great blues performers, and he set about to sing like them, imitating their inflections, their accents, their guttural style. There was and there will always be two Elvises: the nice boy—good to his mother, quiet, a devout Christian, a lover of gospel—and the rocker with the sensual pout, ready to surrender to every excess. He was a perfect image of the Deep South, torn between his religious feelings and his violent urges, his love of God and his appetite for pleasure. The "good" Elvis went to record a love song for his mother. The "wild" Elvis cut loose between takes and bawled out a well-known rock and roll song.

The latter is evidently what attracted the attention of producer Sam Phillips, head of Sun Records. Phillips had learned that increasing numbers of young whites were buying blues and rhythm and blues records. With Elvis he believed he had finally found that rare creature, a white man who sang like he was black, thus creating an infinitely larger commercial potential. In July 1954 he recorded Elvis singing "That's All Right," a popular tune by Arthur Crudup (who would never see much of the money the song brought in). Elvis was supported by studio musicians Scotty Moore (guitar) and Bill Black (bass). These "good old boys" from Tennessee were more used to playing country music but did not mind the rougher idiom of rhythm and blues. This approach of putting muscles on country music was dubbed "rockabilly." Elvis's first and best recordings ("Good Rockin' Tonight," "Milkcow Blues Boogie," and "Mystery Train") attest to this clever combination of black music and cowboy serenades.

## Jerry Lee Lewis, the Killer

With Elvis Presley's first record in black and white—one side black music, the other country—Sun broke a music industry rule: the racial unity of artistic productions. With the introduction of Jerry Lee Lewis on the same label, it broke a second: the avoidance of explicit lyrics. Lewis appropriated

the raw language of black blues singers who were not shy about using metaphors to express passion ("Great Balls of Fire").

Lewis had attended fundamentalist Bible schools before selling his soul to the devil. A remarkable pianist, he had appeared on stage since adolescence, touring markets and fairs with his father; their piano was installed on the back of a flatbed truck. Jerry Lee played a vigorous boogie-woogie. Offstage, the young man tasted the pleasures of the road—alcohol, gambling, women.

The Lewis family was constantly split between religious exaltation and debauchery. Lewis's cousin, the famous televangelist Jimmy Swaggart, is as celebrated for his fiery sermons as for losing his way in the shady sections of town. In the Lewises' congregation, the Pentecostal Assembly of God Church (which Elvis also attended), the parishioners sang until they fell into a trance. They spoke in tongues and beat themselves, while confessing to all sorts of base acts, particularly sexual ones. And no sooner did they leave the church than they resumed their old habits—the trips to go-go bars, the binges, and the poker parties: "Whole Lotta Shakin' Goin' On."

A RELIGIOUS
OAKLAND AU
SUN. MAR
Fea

## White Country and Western Music Meets Black Blues

The craziness of rock and roll life, however, did not infect all of its performers. Compared to the escapades of a Jerry Lee Lewis or a Little Richard, the life of a Carl Perkins or a Bill Haley seems very settled. Perkins was part of the Sun stable before Lewis arrived. A down-to-earth country musician, Perkins had no problem slightly modifying the rhythm of his music to write more rock and roll–type songs like "Blue Suede Shoes." He joined Elvis—who borrowed the song from him and made it a hit— and Jerry Lee Lewis as one of the premier early rock and rollers.

Like other musicians of this

Little Richard (below) was torn between the church and the street.

generation, Perkins followed the
path traced by Hank Williams,
a true legend of country music.
Hank Williams's music, with its blues
strains, captured the spirit—if not
the letter—of rock and roll and broke
with the canons of traditional country
music. While Williams was declared

**BILL HALEY**
**AND HIS COMETS**

persona non grata at the
staid Grand Ole Opry
in Nashville, those
up north in the big cities
paid little attention to a
controversy engendered by
what they perceived as
some backward country
folk clinging to the old
ideas of racial segregation.
And, in any case, they
preferred Bill Haley
and His Comets.

### Rock Around the Clock

From the
beginning
of the
fifties,
Bill Haley,
a former disc
jockey, blended
rhythm and blues hits
into his repertoire of
country and western classics.
Inevitably, the new sounds
met with a favorable response
from young audiences,
even though—to satisfy the
morality guidelines established
by a puritanical white society—
he sanitized the contents of
some of his songs; somewhat
obscene in Joe Turner's original

The acrobatic
contortions of rock
and roll dances were
descended from black
dances like the boogie-
woogie, the black
bottom, and the shimmy.
This physical abandon
did little to enhance the
reputation of rock in
traditionalists' minds.

ALAN D

THE TREN

version, "Shake, Rattle and Roll" was transformed by Bill Haley into an innocuous teenage ditty. But the rhythm remained, and the term "rock" soon found itself associated with a series of songs that spread the new musical message far and wide.

**THE NEWEST BIGGEST ROCK'N'ROLL MOVIE OF ALL!**

In 1955 movies were passionate about the new phenomenon of rock and roll and spread images of its creators around the world.

**ALAN FREED**

**LITTLE RICHARD   DAVE APPELL AND HIS APPLEJACKS**

Bill Haley (above) and promoter Alan Freed are often credited with the invention of the term "rock 'n' roll."

The famous "Rock Around the Clock," recorded in April 1954, holds a key position in the story of this music. The song's importance would be measured the next year, when it appeared on the soundtrack of the newly released film *Blackboard Jungle*. Thus began a strange life for Bill Haley and His Comets. These chubby, overgrown teenagers, these easy-going nice guys who let loose with black rhythms, found themselves speaking for rebellious youth. Their concerts turned into riots; their names appeared on the leather jackets of rebels the world over.

If rock music aroused such passion on its own, what would happen when its performers also adopted the image of potentially dangerous rebels?

### Wild Escapades

Despite his appearance and his posturing on stage, Elvis didn't scare anyone. He had become "acceptable" since his signing with RCA, where, under the control of his manager "Colonel" Tom Parker, he recorded dreamy ballads ("Love Me Tender," "Crying In the Chapel"). But Gene Vincent, Eddie Cochran, and, a little later, Vince Taylor were more threatening. These tough guys were worthy heirs to Brando's motorcycle gangs and lived up to rock and roll's

Eddie Cochran (below) shortly before his death in a car accident in 1960.

reputation for excess and violence propagated by the media. In black leather from head to toe, they frightened parents. Gene Vincent ("Be-Bop-a-Lula") and Eddie Cochran ("Summertime Blues") recharged the dissident spirit of rock and roll. Their style, their image, and even their clothes became an inspiration for many young Americans.

When Buddy Holly (left) died in 1959, rock lost one of its most prolific composers.

Although his appearance as a bespectacled student was more reassuring, Buddy Holly was not any less of a rebel. He turned his back on traditional country music, adding percussion and a beat borrowed from rhythm and blues. With his band, the Crickets, Buddy the Texan gave his seal of approval to rockabilly. His great hits, both in 1957, "That'll Be the Day" and "Peggy Sue," heralded a prolific career, but Holly died tragically at twenty-eight on 3 February 1959 in a plane crash that also took the life of singer Ritchie Valens, the immortal composer of "La Bamba."

Gene Vincent and His Blue Caps (below). The rockabilly "bad boy" was the last rebel of the golden age of the pioneers.

The year was 1955. Parents discovered with dismay their children's new look, which featured slicked-back hair like James Dean's and Elvis Presley's. Teenagers smoked, dressed in blue jeans and leather jackets, and were swept away by the new dances. They flirted and drove convertibles. The strong wind of change, imagination, rebellion, and freedom started in the United States and then blew over the whole Western world.

## CHAPTER II
# THE INVENTION OF THE TEENAGER

Teenagers led the way at the dawn of the fifties. Young Americans wanted to be free. Rock and roll replaced jazz and country music on the jukebox. The record industry had discovered the teenage world.

In 1955 teenagers had economic power, often accompanied by a consumer frenzy equal to that of their parents. They created a new market, which from that time on was flooded with products made especially for their consumption: brand-name leather jackets and the Brando T-shirt, the Thunderbird and the Corvette of the Hollywood playboys, films and Marvel comics. And, of course, records. The 45 rpm single had just made its appearance, and the portable record player allowed teenagers to take over the

The first rock and roll singers left their imprint on street style. One found teenagers sporting Eddie Cochran hairstyles, Buddy Holly jackets, and Carl Perkins blue suede shoes.

world of sound. Until then, to play music they had been dependent on the good mood of their fathers, who were usually in charge of the cumbersome record player enthroned in the family room.

In those carefree and economically developing times, the media, sociologists, and parents suddenly discovered a new phenomenon: the teenager.

The new rock and roll hits gradually replaced the old standards. Thanks to the jukebox one could hear rock in all the teenage hangouts.

From its debut, rock and roll expressed itself in dance—at parties, in clubs, and at concerts. Opposite below: The Platters, who had a string of hits in the fifties.

## The Time of Ballads

Songs reflecting the state of their souls became the primary means of expression for teenagers. Records alternated rapid rock cuts and languorous slow songs perfect for dancing and picking up girls. Little by little, the themes inherited from the blues—solitude, abandonment, bad luck, desperation (Elvis Presley, "Heartbreak Hotel")—ceded their place to inconsequential ballads and rhythmic word games (Gene Vincent, "Be-Bop-a-Lula"). The "doo-wop" sound of black groups, a syncopated form of rhythm and blues noted for its astonishing harmonies and for its fervor, had been popular since the middle of the forties.

Hundreds of groups, heirs to classic vocal groups like the Ink Spots, took their shot at the hit parade. The best known remain the Coasters ("Yakety Yak"), the Drifters ("On Broadway"), the Five Satins ("In the Still of the Night"), the Moonglows, the Penguins, the Cadillacs, the Olympics, the Flamingos, and, above all, the Platters with their long series of hit songs ("Only You," "The Great Pretender," "Smoke Gets in Your Eyes").

Groups of lyricists and composers wrote ballads especially for the teenage market. Songwriting teams like Mort Shuman/Doc Pomus, Jerry Leiber/Mike Stoller, and Gerry Goffin/Carole King were famous for writing a number of small masterpieces of adolescent romance, all marked by false hope, flowery poetry, and a penchant for silliness. Some texts verged on the absurd,

38

In the fifties "cruising" was the favorite pastime of teenagers who discovered both the freedom made possible by the automobile and the freedom of rock and roll. In the sun-filled states of the South and the West, the clear preference was for convertibles (left).

like "Surfin' Bird," based on the Rivingtons' songs but performed by the Trashmen. Twenty years later some bands in the New York punk rock scene would be inspired by this stripped-down rock and roll.

## Chuck Berry: Duck Walks and Guitar Riffs

The development of local radio stations and the exponential growth in the record market conferred on disc jockeys an increasingly important place in the structure of the music business; they now had the power of life and death over an artist's work. Some were tempted by contractual agreements that paid them large sums of money in exchange for repeatedly broadcasting certain songs.
Promoter and DJ

Heir to a long, popular tradition, Chuck Berry's stage show was very suggestive. His famous "duck walk" (left) was adopted later by admiring white musicians like George Thorogood and Keith Richards.

Alan Freed, for example, realizing the potential of young composer-lyricist Chuck Berry, insisted that the musician share with him the profits of his first songs. In exchange, Freed played and promoted them on the air, and in this manner "Maybellene" reached the hit parade in 1955.

This song, like the majority of those written by Berry, dealt

More than the movies of the time, rock and roll reflected the desire of a generation striving to free itself from all prohibitions—especially those regarding sex. After childhood, but before adulthood, adolescence was that difficult in-between age.

N-BETWEEN AGE

with an aspect of the adolescent world—in this case, the automobile. Others evoked school ("School Day"), hanging out on Saturday night ("No Particular Place to Go"), and feelings about growing up ("Almost Grown"). Many of the lyrics could be read as social commentaries on the era, written with the verve and the sly, innuendo-filled humor of a blues singer well acquainted with the world.

Fascinated by Muddy Waters, Berry had no trouble slightly modifying the blues sound to fashion what would

pajama party

become the definitive rock and roll rhythm. His varied stage performances—featuring his famous duck walk—allowed him to escape stylistic traps such as the ones that caught his colleague Bo Diddley. Berry would remain famous for his series of guitar riffs repeated in tune after tune, and his rhythmic energy was widely imitated.

A well-bred, late-fifties copy of Elvis Presley, Ricky Nelson (below) wrote several unforgettable songs like "Hello Mary Lou."

## Rock and Roll Was Immensely Popular at the End of the Fifties

Rock and roll, a mélange of gospel, rhythm and blues, and country and western, broke into multiple categories. There was a world of difference between, for example, the sweet Paul Anka and a sinning pastor like Little Richard. Paul Anka personified a generation of new rock and roll stars. Even with the phenomenal success of songs like "Diana," he gave the impression of a being a nice guy—inoffensive, reassuring, and respectable—as did those "sweet-faced" early rockers like Ricky Nelson ("Hello Mary Lou") and the Everly Brothers ("Claudette," by Roy Orbison). The Everlys revived a vocal style based on rich harmonies that had been popular in the thirties and forties. Their lessons were learned by other groups, as would be seen a short time later with the Beach Boys and the Beatles.

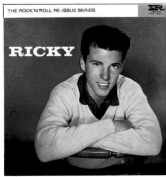

Little Richard—a flamboyant homosexual—had an entirely different image. He furiously played pure rock and roll piano, complete with moves as acrobatic as Jerry Lee Lewis's. But occasional work as a preacher showed through in such spirited compositions as "Lucille" and "Long Tall Sally." Little Richard (Richard Wayne Penniman) perfectly embodied two poles of rock.

Little Richard (right) proclaimed himself "the king of rock and roll," like Elvis Presley. A jealous guardian of his title, he forbade his companions to dress like him. In 1965 Jimi Hendrix was dismissed from the band for forgetting the rules. Thoroughly eccentric, Little Richard abandoned music in 1957 to dedicate himself to selling Bibles. He would return to the stage, however, his extravagant personality still intact.

### Disaster

Toward the end of the fifties, rock and roll seemed to have lost its initial vitality. Its founding fathers had all been struck down by fate—often with a helping hand from the Establishment. In the most shocking case of all, Little Richard, the man who summed up the philosophy of rock with the immortal phrase "A-wop-bop-aloo-bop-a-lop-bam-boom," abandoned rock and roll temporarily in 1957 to become Pastor Penniman.

The year 1958 began with Elvis Presley's departure for the army. "Colonel" Tom Parker had finally tamed the King's rebellious image, and from this point on Elvis had to behave like the rest of the world— to reassure America and, at the same time, to enhance his commercial potential. If Elvis was not totally lost to rock (he still sang pretty ballads), the myth he incarnated was definitely over.

From now on, he would be—for the media, at least—a good family man, married to the daughter of his army colonel and working ardently under the direction of his manager. What did it matter if the work in question consisted of an uninterrupted series of worthless films?

This year also saw the premature end of Jerry Lee Lewis's career. To start with, his marriage to his thirteen-year-old cousin Myra did not endear the media to him. During a successful tour in England, he was brought down with arrows shot by the prudish English press. From that time on he would have to content himself with playing country music, only occasionally lighting up with feeble flashes of his old brilliance.

## The Revenge of Uncle Sam

The next year, 1959, was even more catastrophic. This was the year of Buddy Holly's plane accident; it also marked Chuck Berry's descent into hell. Puritan America had had its eye on Berry for a while— a black man at the top of the hit parade! And one who spoke to teenagers so suggestively! The opportunity to catch him presented itself when he broke a federal law prohibiting the crossing of a state line in the company of a

minor. He claimed that nothing had happened, that the girl had lied about her age, and that his trial was rigged for racist reasons, but, finally, at the end of a long trial and an appeal, he was sentenced to three years in prison. He served two years. The early success of the Beatles and the Rolling Stones can be seen as tributes to his work and helped rehabilitate him in the eyes of the public.

In 1960 fate struck still more pioneers of rock. The taxi taking Eddie Cochran and Gene Vincent to the airport after a successful English concert smashed into a truck. Cochran was killed instantly, and Vincent escaped but was left seriously handicapped.

Middle America relaxed; it could now return to the old values. Already, in small towns people burned records and hung posters calling for boycotts of stations broadcasting the music that had launched the rock and roll movement.

All those who had stood as indomitable rebels were now either toeing the line or dead. The Establishment could only offer antiseptic singers—like Frankie Avalon, Bobby Rydell, and Fabian—respectable, pale imitations of rockers, standard show-business products focusing on the most inoffensive teenage themes. For the time being the torrid lyrics inherited from the tradition of the blues ceded their place to shallow ditties.

However, rock had left its imprint on the subconscious of an entire generation. With its raw energy, its coolness, and its openness, rock allowed

What would Jerry Lee Lewis and Chuck Berry (left) have become if fate hadn't been against them? Would they have eclipsed Elvis Presley? Berry's influence turned out to be much more durable than the King's in that the majority of British groups of the sixties, notably the Beatles and the Rolling Stones, started their careers by performing his songs. The chord progressions he devised in the fifties still serve as the reference point for all apprentice rockers.

Throwing out the years of power exercised by old, corrupt, and obscurantist politicians, in 1960 young America elected to the presidency a man with the profile of a star: John F. Kennedy. His assassination in 1963 coincided with the emergence of the protest song, the first sign of rock's anti-establishment activity.

young people to escape the great postwar ice age. In celebrating youth and its hopes, it had in one sense prepared the way for John F. Kennedy's election in November 1960.

## Teenyboppers and Bobby-Soxers

Women were practically absent from the ranks of the pioneers of rock and roll. Only Brenda Lee would be part of the early story with "Dynamite" in 1958 and "I'm Sorry" in 1960. Hers was a rare example of a successful female solo career in a world dominated by men. The female role models of this period, such as Brigitte Bardot, were to be found in the world of movies, particularly French cinema. Rock was a man's business, because men alone could indulge in tough-guy poses, beyond the taboos of sex and drugs. In this clearly defined universe, Brenda Lee presented the image of a slightly nervous and terribly virginal college girl. Music would evolve at the beginning of the sixties, thanks to two Pygmalions of shock: Phil Spector in California and George "Shadow" Morton in New York. Spector invented the "wall of sound," a recording technique that earned him an uninterrupted succession of spots at the top of the hit parade. With a nod to the modern age, the term is associated with the speed records of the first jet airplanes and with breaking the sound

...*presenting the*

RON

*featuring* VERO

BE MY BABY •
BABY
CHA
WHAT'D I SAY
WHE

Producer Phil Spector married the leader of the Ronettes, Ronnie (below).

# ETTES

## ICA

barrier. Spector gathered as many musicians and singers as he could fit in his studio. By playing with echo chambers and multitracking, he obtained an orchestral intensity that recalled that of a church packed to the rafters on a gospel Sunday.

The artists Phil Spector produced were primarily female groups, beauties like the Crystals ("Da Doo Ron Ron") and the Ronettes ("Be My Baby"), whose leader, "Ronnie" (Veronica), he married. With Spector and his creation of a sonic language specific to each artist, rock production definitively left the Dark Ages.

At the same time "Shadow" Morton made a name for himself as another pioneer of production with his favorite group, the Shangri-las. They were white, lived in Queens, New York, and displayed a far more provocative image than, for instance, the innocent Brenda Lee. These girls sang of complicated—and tragic—love affairs with motorcycle gang members ("Leader of the Pack") and, in real life, led an existence worthy of a Jerry Lee Lewis.

### Rock and Roll Arrived in England

Since 1956 rock and roll had been very successful in Europe. It was spread by the jukebox and by the movies—*Blackboard Jungle,* with Bill Haley's music, and the first films of Elvis Presley (*King Creole* and *Jailhouse Rock,* the only ones worthy of interest). Radio Luxembourg, with its huge radio transmitters, broadcast the music around the continent. Tours by

They were called teenyboppers or bobby-soxers. The girls of rock were pretty and a little seductive, perhaps, but not provocative. Social pressure prohibited them from assuming the suggestive poses of their male counterparts.

Fats Domino, Little Richard, Eddie Cochran, and Gene Vincent generated in their wake a passion that translated itself into the creation of numerous imitations, particularly in England. Not only did England share a language with the United States, of course, but it had a working-class base with a strong and rebellious identity. A new character appeared on the European scene: the rocker.

In the 1950s whatever came from America fascinated Europeans. American clothes, films, records, and even attitudes constituted symbols of freedom; identifying with this message, European teenagers developed an intense desire to appropriate. Thus, the first English rock singers conformed to their American models quite closely—so much so that they were like copies. One could identify Elvis or Gene Vincent in Tommy Steele ("Singing the Blues"), Billy Fury, Marty Wilde, or Rory Storm. The imagery of rock revolved completely around violence, more theatrical than real, which, when it was mixed with British eccentricity, gave rise to a Wee Willie Harris, whose dyed red pile of abundantly brilliantined hair would have appealed to Little Richard.

In Great Britain at the end of the fifties, the "teddy boys" (above) adopted elegant attire inspired by the standards of King Edward VII. Coming together in clubs, teddy boys added a new dimension to rockabilly, which had just landed on that side of the Atlantic.

Another Richard very quickly won the public's favor. Cliff Richard shared many of the same inclinations as his namesake, but in a minor way, remaining true to the "coolness" displayed by white American rockers. He was certainly a good singer ("Livin' Doll"), but he

Rock 'n' roll was the last dance in which bodies touched. With the twist, popularized by Chubby Checker in his famous "Let's Twist Again," everyone invented their own steps and danced alone. Pope John XXIII condemned this trend when it made its appearance in Europe at the beginning of the sixties. Other dances of the same type followed in a cascade: the madison, the jerk, the mashed potato.

was above all a stylist inspired by the "soft" Presley of the Parker years. His performances, however, never overshadowed that of the Shadows, who played with him. Sometimes led by their guitarist, Hank Marvin, a Buddy Holly imitator, the Shadows recaptured the sound of the Ventures, a Seattle group. At the end of the fifties, the Ventures had introduced a new style of electric guitar, brilliant, individual, with a distinctive tremolo sound. The most famous songs by Hank Marvin and the Shadows—without Cliff Richard—("Apache," "Kon Tiki") attracted the attention of a public previously hesitant in its response to amplified instruments. Watching Hank Marvin and the Shadows on British

"ROCK AND ROLL"

HENRY CORDING

Exclusivité Fontana
45 SFD. 460.518 ME

1. Rock and Roll-Mops
2. Dis-moi que tu m'aimes Rock
3. Rock-Hoquet
4. Va t'faire cuire un Oeuf, Man!

et la voix de HENRI SALVADOR

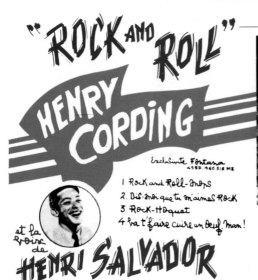

French musicians Boris Vian (above) and Henri Salvador (below) were devoted to jazz but did not ignore rock and roll.

television, a number of future "guitar heroes" saw the birth of their dreams.

### The Birth of "Yogurt"

On the European continent, in France, rock and roll was at first perceived as a gag, a new manifestation of the impulsive American character. Musicians with strong roots in jazz, like Boris Vian and Henri Salvador, saw in rock a drifting away from the vividness of the blues. They translated their feelings into deliberately idiotic songs like "Rock 'n' Roll Mops" or "Va T'Faire Cuire un Oeuf, Man" ("Go Cook an Egg, Man" or "Get Lost, Man"). None of the early French rockers had an easy time. No one took them seriously, except themselves.

Many French people, however, were ready to buy the American 45s they found in NATO base PXs or the rare French record stores that distributed them. For want of other source materials, several French singers launched into the great adventure of rock and roll by adapting, often colorfully, the gestures and the words of the originals. Thus "yogurt" was born, a phonetic caricature of English that tried to recreate an English that very few really understood. The words and meaning didn't matter. Only the spirit counted—and the attitude.

Danyel Gérard was the first champion of this somewhat specialized form of rock. His late-fifties shows recalled those of Johnnie Ray, a pre-Elvis performer who mimicked poses that imitated practices found in American black churches. The press didn't let Gérard get away with it, describing him as a "suffocating singer." Then the army grabbed him and destroyed his fledgling career by calling him to serve his country.

The appearance of rock and roll in France did not please everyone. Some laughed at it; others tried to suppress it. And the concerts turned into mayhem. The Palais des Sports in Paris was devastated several times, notably in 1961 during performances by Eddie Mitchell et Ses Chaussettes Noires and then again when the band joined Vince Taylor.

## A New Dance and a New Kind of Hoodlum

In 1960 the action was situated around the Golf Drouot club in Paris. All of rock's upper crust paraded through there: Johnny Hallyday ("Souvenirs, Souvenirs"), a child of the theater who modeled himself on the personalities of James Dean and Elvis Presley; Eddie Mitchell et Ses Chaussettes Noires (and His Black Socks), inspired by Gene Vincent's Blue Caps; Danny Boy et les Penitents (and the Penitents), Danny Logan et les Pirates (and the Pirates), Long Chris et les Daltons (and the Daltons). Many of these names were dug up from westerns and

*TWIST*

comic books, a key part of French teenage culture. In the south of France, Dick Rivers et Ses Chats Sauvages (and His Wild Cats) picked up fragments of rock and roll from the American base in Villefranche.

Soon the French discovered the twist, given a place of honor by Chubby Checker. It was

Eddie Mitchell's Chaussettes Noires and Dick Rivers's Chats Sauvages vied for the favor of the French public. It is to Rivers's credit that "Twist à Saint Tropez" is considered one of the rare masterpieces of the first wave of French rock.

a true revolution for dancers: After its arrival partners did not touch.

The French media—like the American—was only too glad to focus on the occasional outburst of violence that came as a reminder that this rock and roll movement was born of an immense frustration with a terribly restrictive political and social era. There were many gleeful reports of the devastation of a concert hall during a concert by the Chaussettes Noires (at this time led by Vince Taylor), and other articles raised the specter of a new kind of hoodlum—called the *blousons noirs*—leatherclad bullies à la Brando who terrified the French middle class.

Gone were the old gangs; France had discovered a new generation of toughs.

The Golf Drouot club in Paris saw a parade of the stars of the day and the hopes of tomorrow. A kind of amateur talent show was born here in front of a jukebox playing the original versions of rock and roll songs, which were remade into "yogurt."

## "Hello Friends"

Show business moguls in France quickly realized the commercial potential represented by the new generation, and they launched band after band—as well as a series of solo male and female singers—without regard for their talent. They Frenchified everything that crossed the Atlantic. While it was necessary to respect government-enforced protectionist quotas, the brand-new station Radio Europe 1 did manage to broadcast original rock as well as the "translated" version.

With his radio show, "Salut Les Copains" ("Hello Friends"), host Daniel Filipacchi—originally a jazz critic—recognized the importance of his young audience and decided to create a magazine for this public. Conceived in June 1962 in the same spirit as the broadcast, the magazine permitted French teenagers to uncover a mirror that reflected both themselves and their ideals—Johnny Hallyday, Sylvie Vartan, Françoise Hardy, Richard Anthony, Sheila—and was such a success that it allowed Filipacchi to lay the foundations of what would become a communications empire.

## The Advent of "Ye-Ye"

**VIENS DANSER LE TWIST**
**Partie 1 en Français**
**Partie 2 en Anglais**
**DOUCE VIOLENCE**
**Il FAUT SAISIR SA CHANCE**
**NOUS, QUAND ON S'EMBRASSE**
**TOI QUI REGRETTES**
**AVEC UNE POIGNÉE DE TERRE**
**TU PEUX LA PRENDRE**

At the dawn of the sixties, rock became so popular that it upset the French Establishment, which was anxious to avoid social destabilization, and all rock concerts were banned. Little by little, the hardliners were isolated: the *blousons noirs* became passé, banished to the working-class suburbs.

A new phenomenon appeared: "ye-ye," sentimental, watered-down pop music, with all subversive elements and any potential of revolt removed. In this sense events followed the course they had taken in the United States several years earlier. The only difference was that it took France until 1968 to upset this new order of things. The U.S. and England would experience a faster social evolution, and rock set the pace.

In 1961 French rock groups compensated for a dearth of talent with enthusiasm, and the liveliness of the performances made one forget the second-rate music.

*nny* **HALLYDAY**

To the foreigner, Johnny Hallyday personified French rock and roll. One of his first 33 rpm ten-inch albums celebrated the arrival of the twist in France (left and above).

In the United States rock and roll came from the provinces. And in England, too, part of rock's allure was its distinct freshness: The Beatles emerged, with their Northern accents and the naïveté of their songs. The imagination of a new generation caught fire, and thousands of other groups rushed in.

CHAPTER III

# ROCK WITH AN ENGLISH ACCENT

In Brighton, England, rockers (left) and the mods of Carnaby Street went head to head during the spring of 1964. The mods came out on top in this dispute over clothing, music, and style.

Liverpool 1960. Rock and roll was established in the working-class milieu of sailors, dockers, and bus drivers. Little by little, local groups abandoned "skiffle," a kind of hillbilly blues born in the Depression years in America and later assimilated in England. Lonnie Donegan, its most famous practitioner, was taught by Chris Barber, the leading light of "trad," the British version of the New Orleans sound and a central figure at the Marquee Club in London. John Lennon was one of Donegan's most devoted followers at the end of the fifties.

## Liverpool and the Beatles

In 1957 Lennon asked Paul McCartney to join his group, the Quarrymen, after having heard him perform a spirited version of Eddie Cochran's "Twenty Flight Rock." About a year later McCartney brought in his younger

# THE BEATLES

Brian Epstein (below left) discovered the Beatles in their regular Liverpool club, the Cavern. Attracted first by the personality of John Lennon, Epstein had a decisive influence on the group. His first requirement would be to eliminate the slightly seedy rocker look of the four young men, dressing them up in much more banal outfits than their old leather jackets. Moving into the mainstream, the Beatles recorded their first hits. "Please Please Me" (the single was released in January 1963) was a clear call for affection to which there was a tremendous public response.

friend George Harrison. Stuart Sutcliffe then joined to play bass, and the group was completed by Pete Best, a drummer. The Quarrymen (the name referred to the Quarry Bank School, which John attended) became Johnny and the Moondogs, then the Silver Beatles— these lengthy names were in honor of Buddy Holly and the Crickets. When the group finally agreed on the name of the Beatles in 1960, it was still a tribute to Holly, with a bit of John Lennon–style wordplay on the word "beat."

The band often played at the Cavern, a small underground club in Liverpool. They also toured Germany, performing in the disreputable clubs of the Reeperbahn in Hamburg. There, the group's bassist, Stuart Sutcliffe (who died a few months later), fell in love with photographer Astrid Kirchherr. It was she who had

Australian photographer Robert Freeman posed the Beatles like true icons. The picture above, taken in 1963, which appeared on the cover of their second British album, would remain symbolic of the Beatles' style. Their haircuts marked the starting point for the liberation of hairstyles for all rock artists to come.

suggested that the Beatles adopt their "French cut" hair style, a kind of wink at French New Wave cinema actors.

Brian Epstein, the biggest record dealer in Liverpool, became the band's manager in late 1961. His first action was to replace Pete Best with Richard Starkey—known as Ringo Starr—the ex-drummer for Rory Storm and the Hurricanes. The magic quartet was now in place.

### Beatlemania Sweeps the World

Their first album (*Please Please Me*, May 1963) reflected the band's influences: vocal harmonies borrowed from the Everly Brothers, guitar riffs taken from Chuck Berry, spirited melodies recalling Buddy Holly, and a falsetto straight from Little Richard. The lyrics, performed in a delightful Liverpudlian accent, addressed themselves directly to the audience ("Love Me Do," "I Wanna Be Your Man," "Hold Me Tight," "I Wanna Hold Your Hand"). The more the Beatles' popularity grew, the more often songs signed "Lennon-McCartney" replaced the American standards of rock and rhythm and blues.

The Beatles' success encouraged Brian Epstein to launch a string of groups under the aegis of his company, Northern Songs. Known as the Mersey Beat or the Mersey Sound (after the river that flows through Liverpool), this movement brought to the stage, among others, Gerry and the Pacemakers and Cilla Black—one of the rare female performers of the period.

NT TO HOLD YOUR HAND • IT WON'T BE LONG

NNA BE YOUR MAN • TILL THERE WAS YOU

The Beatles (left) were often forced to pose with backdrops of dubious taste and would soon tire of the servitude imposed on them by promotional campaigns. Their fans ignored these torments and noisily showed their enthusiasm during concerts (below). The music and the words of the songs were lost in the pandemonium. What did it matter? What counted was seeing the Fab Four.

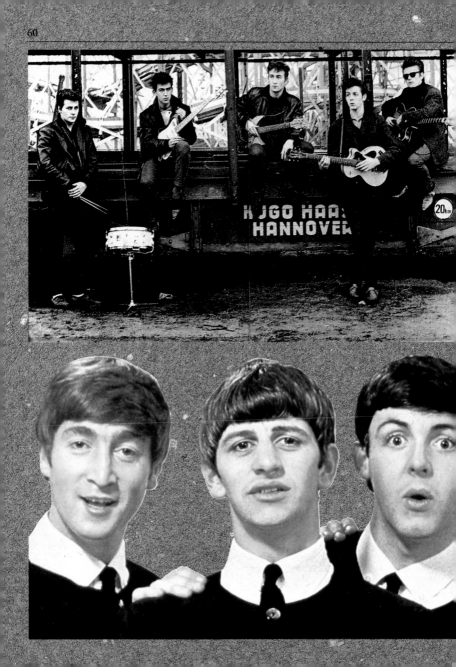

THE **BEATLES** ARE AT **THE CAVERN** TUESDAY NIGHT 19TH FEBRUARY 1963 BE EARLY

In 1961 the Beatles went to Hamburg. Photographer Astrid Kirchherr took their portrait (opposite above) and fell in love with bassist Stuart Sutcliffe. At the time of the photograph there were five Beatles (left to right: Pete Best, George Harrison, John Lennon, Paul McCartney, and Stuart Sutcliffe). The group of three guitarists (left) recalled the Shadows, the obligatory reference point of English rock in this period. John Lennon was the only one who possessed an instrument of any value, a Rickenbacker that would later become the Beatles' emblematic guitar. Two years later, reduced to a quartet, they completely revised their look (below). The black-jacketed toughs of Hamburg had become chic young men. By this point they were already very popular, but they returned to Liverpool to play at the Cavern, the little club where they began. Despite its fame, the Cavern would be demolished. However, a museum, statues, and several street names perpetuate the memory of the Fab Four in their hometown.

In 1963 the Beatles turned a corner, and the craziness of Beatlemania began. Their concerts were chaos. People dressed like them and cut their hair like them. The tremendous willingness for change that was in the air—the desire to throw out old Victorian England completely—was incarnated in the Fab Four. Their 45s sold in the millions. Soon Great Britain was too narrow to contain Beatlemania, and the phenomenon left to conquer the rest of Europe and then the United States.

## Blues with a British Accent

During this time, there was an influx of blues influence in London as musicians Big Bill Broonzy, Muddy Waters, and Sonny Boy Williamson performed. Mick Jagger, Charlie Watts, Jack Bruce, and Ginger Baker— in fact, all the key names who would create rock music in the coming years—heard American blues and also gravitated toward British blues musicians Alexis Korner and Cyril Davies.

Like Korner, John Mayall worked hard to respect the spirit and the letter of the blues masters. Eric Clapton, Peter Green, John McVie, Mick Taylor—all "graduates" of Mayall's Bluesbreakers band—would never forget their lessons. Along with their teacher, they were responsible for the mid-sixties blues boom. And an outgrowth of Alexis Korner's Blues Incorporated, the Rolling Stones (named after a Muddy Waters song) went on to make rock and roll history.

Keith Richards and Mick Jagger had known each other since childhood. They shared with Brian Jones, whom they met at Korner's, a pronounced taste for rhythm and blues in all its forms: the image-filled vitality of street language, a nonchalant attitude, and extravagant hair and dress. Jagger reveled in the pleasure of the music, pushing Presley and his famous swagger into oblivion. The Stones' first manager, Andrew Loog Oldham, encouraged them, thinking that their style would at least distinguish them from the "nice" Beatles.

### Rolling Stones

On their first album (*The Rolling Stones*) the Stones paid an emphatic compliment to those who influenced them, in particular

The first Rolling Stones album (above), released in 1964, was a direct homage to Chuck Berry. The contrast with the Beatles—their real or supposed rivals—was striking. Abandoning their stage costumes and smiles, they followed the advice of their manager, Andrew Loog Oldham: to speak frankly, to make no concessions to photographers, and, under all circumstances, to give the impression of being bored and outraged.

The Rolling Stones in 1964. Left to right: Brian Jones, Charlie Watts, Mick Jagger, and Keith Richards.

Chuck Berry ("Around and Around"), and this recognition allowed Berry to find his audience again after his release from prison. Brian Jones—in fact, the initial impetus of the group—was the most adored in the band, but when tension developed between him and Keith Richards after a bitter fight to establish the instrumental leader of the group, Jones, the weaker, gave up. The Stones' rapid success enflamed

The Rolling Stones (under the table) gave traditionally virtuous England a hard time. Ignoring proper Oxford English, they adopted the clearly cruder slang of Chicago blacks. They often got themselves in trouble: Brian Jones (in shirtsleeves at right) was arrested several times for possession of marijuana. As his musical leadership was contested by Keith Richards and Mick Jagger, Jones progressively withdrew into the background until he quit the group, just before his death in 1969.

the rhythm and blues movement in England. Groups exploded from every corner.

In London the Pretty Things were formed around Dick Taylor, a member of the first Stones lineup. The Yardbirds, a younger, pure blues–based group, saw a parade of three legendary guitarists: Eric Clapton, the first "guitar hero," who was nicknamed God by his fans and left the group when it became popular ("For Your Love"); Jeff Beck, who reinvented the electric guitar by integrating into his technique a sludge of sound—especially fuzz and distortion ("Shapes of Things"); and Jimmy Page, who attended the creation of most of the great hits of the era.

In Newcastle the Animals, with their singer Eric Burdon, followed in the footsteps of John Lee Hooker ("Boom Boom"). In Ireland the group Them, featuring singer Van Morrison, championed a rough rhythm and blues ("Gloria"). They all shared a wild desire to score on the hit parade, where the competition was not always friendly and the stakes were clearly defined: quick fame, quick money, quick sex.

## Mods and Rockers

English rock didn't just sell records. It was a tremendous promotional tool for other products: miniskirts and cosmetics (Mary Quant), hair salons (Vidal Sassoon), boots, costumes. But beyond the emphasis on dress, the entire society was in the process of shifting, turning its back on outdated customs. These upheavals did not please everyone.

Lovers of pure rock and roll saw a degradation of the original message and a weakening of the raw energy of the pioneers of the genre. They maintained that

The Pretty Things (above) could have been as popular as the Rolling Stones. Their leader, Dick Taylor (second from the right), had been part of the Stones during their early stages in 1962. When they became famous in 1965, the Pretty Things went, without a doubt, too far in their provocative image: They sported the longest hair and the most bohemian manners, and the public had a hard time following the rapid decline in their comportment and appearance. Nevertheless, their music was much closer to original rhythm and blues than other English groups'.

distinctive look: exaggerated
pompadours, sideburns,
leather jackets, and big English
motorcycles. Rooted in the 1950s,
the rockers regularly confronted
their opposites, the mods, who were aggressively
up to date with their short hair, French clothes,
and decorated motor scooters. It was Carnaby Street,
the fashionable London district, versus Club 59.
Symbolically, the split between the two movements
occurred in 1962 when Pete Best was dismissed
from the Beatles because of his refusal to change,
to adopt a new image.

First, you had to be cool, aloof. The mods were the
first to claim the use of legally suspect substances,
particularly amphetamines ("purple hearts"), which they
took to enable them to dance all through the weekend.
The long hot summer was punctuated with their pitched
battles against the rockers in the wild clubs of Soho and
on the beaches of Brighton. Inevitably, the mods won.
They discovered economic independence and all its
available pleasures. Their musical tastes tended toward
modern jazz (hence their name) and classic rhythm and
blues, which they danced to on the weekends. The Who,
originally named High Numbers, expressed some of the
mod credos in their songs: "My Generation" with its
swaggering stanzas ("Hope I die before I get old") or
"Pictures of Lily," an ode to masturbation.

In 1963 the
motorcyclists of Club
59 faced off with the
wave of mods perched
on decorated Italian
motor scooters (above).
Added to this contest
of machinery was a
profound difference in
musical taste. The
motorcyclists—or rockers
(opposite above)—
supported the rock and
roll of the fifties, while
the mods preferred the
new English groups,
above all the Who,
whose clothing was
mod in inspiration.

**Who Put The Bomp**

VOLUME 3   NO. 1   HOLLYWOOD, CALIFORNIA   BUY BONDS   FALL 1973   PRICE $1.00

# BRITISH INVASION

**The British Invasion**

Starting in 1964, dozens of English groups arrived in New York eager to gather a maximum of dollars in a minimum of time. The United States was

It's time we exorcise this demon influence over our children

at their mercy. It had not known a similar fervor since the golden days of rock and roll. Welcomed by the media, the Beatles outsmarted every interview trap with humor. Now there were the same scenes of hysteria in the United States as in England—delirious girls, hotels taken by storm, and "authentic" souvenir businesses selling shreds of sheets that were worn around the neck like religious emblems, autographs scribbled by bodyguards, or, on a higher level, tea sets and wallpapers. In the second wave the Rolling Stones provoked similar riots. Mick Jagger's very physical stage performance gave rise to a complete change in the attitude of white American singers. Most of them wanted to imitate his leaps and his catlike poses.

But it was in its impact on society that the "British Invasion" produced its most remarkable effect. Beatnik America recognized itself in these young rebels, especially since they were held in contempt by the Establishment. The entire country was traumatized by John Kennedy's assassination. And the English tornado stimulated the energies of a new generation of artists—rockers, poets, singers—who seemed to be just waiting for this opportunity to express themselves.

More than ten years after the beginning of the British Invasion, *Who Put The Bomp,* an American rock fanzine (opposite), recalled the place the Beatles and the Rolling Stones (below, in concert in 1970) held in it.

In the early sixties, the youth of America underwent a profound moral crisis. The Vietnam War, the civil rights movement, and the corruption of the political and legal system led to strong antiestablishment sentiment and general unrest. Suddenly rock and roll musicians took on an unprecedented role: They became the spokespeople of a generation. In the forefront was Bob Dylan.

RC/I
VICTOR
STEREO
BFL1 0919

## CHAPTER IV
## AN AMERICAN REVOLUTION

After the first wave of protest songs, rock discovered political commitment. Propelled by the music of bands like the Jefferson Airplane, antiestablishment and antiwar activity pervaded college campuses.

The rhythm and blues music that had provided such glorious times for the British mods was created in the hit factories of Motown in Detroit and Stax in Memphis. Motown, founded by Berry Gordy in 1959, produced Marvin Gaye ("Ain't That Peculiar"),

While the Beatles and the Rolling Stones dominated in Europe, America supported such black rhythm and blues artists as Otis Redding (below), Al Green, and the stars of the Motown stable (above).

Smokey Robinson ("I Second that Emotion"), the Temptations ("Ain't Too Proud to Beg"), the Four Tops ("Bernadette"), Stevie Wonder ("Fingertips —Part 2"), the Jackson Five ("ABC"), Diana Ross and the Supremes ("I'm Gonna Make You Love Me"), Martha and the Vandellas ("Dancing in the Streets"), Gladys Knight and the Pips ("I Heard It Through the Grapevine"), and more. In ten years over a hundred Motown songs made number one on the hit parade.

Stax, however, was tough competition. Their

legendary rhythm section—Booker T. Jones (the composer of "Green Onions," at the Hammond organ) and his MGs (who would later play with the Blues Brothers)—accompanied such house artists as Otis Redding ("Try a Little Tenderness"), without doubt one of the great soul singers of his generation, and Sam and Dave ("Hold On, I'm Coming"). Stax enjoyed such a reputation that Atlantic Records, its distributor, recorded some of its own artists, like Wilson Pickett ("In the Midnight Hour"), in the Stax studio.

But of all the black singers, James Brown had the greatest success. Sometimes popular with

Detroit, the automobile capital of America, was the home of Motown, the birthplace of countless hits. One of its stars was the Jackson Five (below, Michael, age eight, is at bottom in the center).

the public, sometimes rejected because of his political activities and his escapades, he was a model showman. Brown was an amazing dancer, constantly inventing new steps (enumerated in his song "Papa's Got a Brand New Bag"). He influenced his American colleagues (like Michael Jackson) as much as he did British pop groups. The Apollo Theater in Harlem, New York, was the scene of many of his greatest performances.

## Gospel: The Unique Crucible

Former preachers like Al Green ("I Can't Get Next to You") or children of pastors like Aretha Franklin ("Respect") learned to sing in church, and in their pop careers they helped maintain a religious current in rock and in rhythm and blues. There are traces of the religious in the lyrics of their songs, with their optimism,

Two superstars of rhythm and blues and soul: Aretha Franklin and James Brown. Aretha Franklin, daughter of the most famous preacher in Detroit, had sung in a gospel choir since childhood. Her voice has retained the imprint of that upbringing; it is full, deep, and strong. Coming from the South, James Brown directed himself toward a very secular rhythm and blues at the beginning of the fifties. An amazing showman, he invented a multitude of new dances copied in clubs the world over. His influence on pop music was considerable, particularly in England where he was venerated as a god by the mods of the sixties.

SEX POWER AND LOVE

JAMES BROWN
From Augusta, Ga.
The ★ The Sex Machine

The man who sings
"MAKE IT FUNKY"
"TRY ME"
"LOST SOMEONE"
'BLACK and PROUD'
"SUPER BAD"
"SOUL POWER"
"SEX MACHINE"
"HOT PANTS"
"ESCAPE-ISM"

their hope for a better world, and their messages bordering on prayer. This feeling has also manifested itself in the fever generated by some concerts, their ritualization, and, in recent years, their focus on great humanitarian causes.

At the beginning of the sixties, this current of devotion found a renewed interest among whites with the protest song. Rooted partially in folk, bluegrass, and blues, as well as in gospel, the movement focused as much on the spiritual as on the political. Led by Pete Seeger and his "Sing Out" revue, folk singers devoted themselves to challenging institutions and consciousness raising in general. The most remarkable performers were Phil Ochs, Eric Andersen, Peter, Paul and Mary, and, above all, Joan Baez and Bob Dylan.

### Bob Dylan: Rock Became Literary

When Bob Dylan's first album appeared in 1962, folk was already in fashion on college campuses. The Kingston Trio

In 1965 Richard Avedon took this beautiful portrait of Joan Baez (above) for her album *Farewell, Angelina*. The title song was written by Bob Dylan (opposite), who was then sharing her life. Labeled "the king and queen of folk" by the media, Dylan and Baez spoke for the hopes of the public.

Joan Baez (left, at the microphone) was always more than a musician. She was a key participant in political events, here speaking against censorship and for the freedom of speech on the Berkeley campus of the University of California in 1963.

("Tom Dooley") and the Brothers Four ("Greenfields") concentrated on poignant songs, rich in vocal harmonies but nonthreatening to the Establishment.

But Dylan made his reputation as a rebel. Born Robert Zimmerman, 24 May 1941, in Duluth, Minnesota, he was influenced early on by the rock and roll of Little Richard, the country and western of Hank Williams, and the whole persona of Woody Guthrie. Everything about Guthrie fascinated him: the writer-hobo precursor of Kerouac, the protest singer who translated the tragedies of ruined farmers and tramps into songs, the social commentator, the wounded hero, the vagabond. The first success of Bob Dylan carried the imprint of this relationship. Dubbed by Pete Seeger the authentic heir to Woody Guthrie, Dylan, who could have contented himself to be the darling of student rebels, established himself as a redresser of wrongs and then became larger than life, a widely imitated prophet.

## Summer of 1965: The Newport Folk Festival

To the great dismay of folk purists, Dylan appeared onstage with an electric guitar, accompanied by the Butterfield Blues Band. It was a typical rock and roll challenge, especially since he seemed to have renounced plaid shirts for a look borrowed from the Beatles.

Dylan continued along his path as an absolute individualist. Encouraged by his producer Tom Wilson, he intensified his exploration of rock in a brilliant two years, 1965–6, marked by three key albums. The half-acoustic,

Bob Dylan's acoustic guitar remained a painful symbol in the hearts of folk lovers. For them, Dylan was the emblematic figure of the protest song, heir to Woody Guthrie, charged with a messianic task, which he never ceased to refuse ("Don't follow leaders!" he wrote in 1965). Purists needed years to accept Dylan's electric arrangements and heated rock and roll exchanges. As if to disconcert his audience again and again, he would periodically return to his original style.

BO

first and only bay area performance

half-electric *Bringing It All Back Home* and *Highway 61 Revisited*, shot through by the lightning streaks of Mike Bloomfield's guitar, were both produced by Wilson and

released in 1965. *Blonde on Blonde* (1966), the first double album in the history of rock, was recorded in Nashville, the mecca of country music. These records were

**saturday, february 22,** 8:30 p.m.

**berkeley community theater**

**admission: $2.50, 3.00, & 3.75**

B ob Dylan concerts sometimes turned unruly. In 1965 at the Newport Folk Festival the audience booed him: He had dared to venture on stage accompanied by a blues-rock group, the Butterfield Blues Band. In the spring of 1966 an equally stormy welcome awaited him

studded with such classic cuts as "Like a Rolling Stone." In the mid-sixties Dylan also toured with the Band, critically acclaimed and influential in their own right.

## The Invention of California

By 1966 America had found a credible

at the Royal Albert Hall in London, where supporters and adversaries of the "new" Dylan confronted each other.

## GIRLS ON THE BEACH

reply to the Beatles: the Beach Boys. The Wilson brothers—Brian, Carl, and Dennis —their cousin Mike Love, and their friend Al Jardine landed their first hit in 1961 with "Surfin'." Dennis was the only surfer in the band, but he persuaded Brian, an enormously talented lyricist and composer, to write songs glorifying the pleasures preferred by his friends: dune buggies, girls, and the beach. The "surf sound" was born at the same time as the myth of a carefree, sunny California, a teenager's green paradise, complete with dragsters and dark suntans. Something in Brian Wilson's songs conveyed the feeling of Chuck Berry circa "School Day." This rhythm, blended with complex vocal harmonies inherited from the Everly Brothers and the

Four Freshmen, propelled the Beach Boys to the head of American groups. Other California bands included the Mamas and the Papas ("California Dreaming"), the Turtles ("Happy Together"), Leaves ("Hey Joe"), Buffalo Springfield (with Stephen Stills and Neil Young, "For What It's Worth"), and the Byrds (with Roger McGuinn and David Crosby, "Eight Miles High").

Los Angeles, of course, didn't tell the whole California story. As the wind of psychedelia began to blow, San Francisco, with its reputation for tolerance, seemed infinitely hipper. And, mid-decade, the term "hippies" was born. At the beginning, hippies, heirs to the beatniks, were primarily intellectuals who turned their back on the Establishment's power game and competition. The news gradually spread across America

The Beach Boys (opposite) strutted about, posing as surfers only for the camera. In reality, only the drummer, Dennis Wilson (first in line) surfed. His brother Brian (last in line) was the soul of the group. He lived by himself and composed his hymns to the pleasures of adolescence—girls, jalopies, and surfing—based on Dennis's adventures.

In 1967 Joan Baez participated in a protest in front of an armed forces recruitment center in Oakland, California. A pacifist, she advocated nonviolence.

that something was brewing in San Francisco. More and more young people arrived every day seeking welcome in communities that were already too crowded.

There were more than 500,000 "runaways" during the "Summer of Love" (1967), drawn by a perspective on life that differed from what was offered in some midwestern suburb. Two products awaited them: acid—LSD—and rock. The two mixed happily, with songs by local groups like the Jefferson Airplane and the Grateful Dead extolling the merits of acid "trips."

## Psychedelic Rock

The Grateful Dead, formed in late 1965, was wreathed in the glory of the pioneers: Jerry Garcia, spokesman of the group, was nicknamed

BILL GRAHAM PF

"Captain Trips." A great admirer of French jazz musician Django Reinhardt, he developed a style of rapid, incisive guitar playing inherited from his past as a banjo player in a jug band (a small acoustic folk group playing makeshift instruments.)

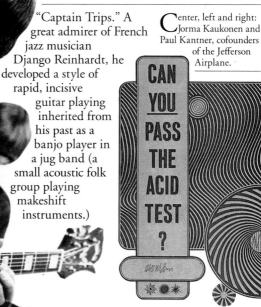

Center, left and right: Jorma Kaukonen and Paul Kantner, cofounders of the Jefferson Airplane.

CAN YOU PASS THE ACID TEST ?

The Grateful Dead and the Jefferson Airplane toured across North America in 1967 (poster below).

THE SAN FRANCISCO SCENE

RONTO
To
L·AUG 5
GRATEFUL DEAD
LIGHT SHOW BY HEAD LIGHTS
CENTRE
• Mats. Wed & Sat.     Box Office Open from 11 a.m. to 9pm.     J GARDNER

Other members brought with them their individual sounds: Bob Weir, rock and roll; Ron "Pigpen" McKernan, rhythm and blues; and Phil Lesh, tonal research. Drummer Bill Kreutzmann completed the group. In 1966 the Dead settled down in the eye of the storm on Ashbury Street and participated in all the

The Family Dog (right) was the biggest hippie among the concert promoters.

QUICKSILVER MESSENGER SERVICE
BIG BROTHER & THE HOLDING COMPANY
THE GRATEFUL DEAD
THE GRASSROOTS
SUNSHINE

great events of the area, like the famous Human Be-In held in Golden Gate Park in January 1967 and free concerts bringing together the best local groups— Quicksilver Messenger Service ("Happy Trails"), Big Brother and the Holding Company (with its singer Janis

In 1966 San Francisco's Fillmore Auditorium entrusted the creation of its concert posters to the best graphic artists of the day. They tried to outdo each other in presenting the local talent (left and below) as well as touring bands (opposite below, the Yardbirds).

BIG BROTHER AND THE HOLDING COMPANY
FILLMORE AND GEARY · S:00 P.M. FILLMORE AUDITORIUM
SUNDAY FEB. 19

THE FAMILY DOG PRESENTS THE *JEFFERSON AIRPLANE*

Joplin, "Cheap Thrills"), the Charlatans ("Charlatans"), and the Jefferson Airplane.

The Airplane debuted as a folk-rock group around the same time as the Dead, making their first recording in 1966 with a banjo (Marty Balin), acoustic guitar (Paul Kantner), bass (Bob Harvey), drums (Skip Spence), lead guitar (Jorma Kaukonen), and a singer, Signe Anderson, who quickly ceded her place to Grace Slick. With its second album, *Surrealistic Pillow*, the Airplane established itself as a leading voice of the hippie movement, its poetic lyrics evoking hallucinogens, free love, and social commitment. The band didn't escape the notice of Bill Graham, creator of the legendary concerts at the Fillmore, and the Jefferson Airplane became a major attraction on the San Francisco scene.

Faced with such success, the big recording companies raced each other to sign psychedelic artists. This would be the chance for Big Brother; for Carlos Santana, the Chicano guitarist ("Evil Ways"); and for Country Joe McDonald and the Fish, a band composed of politicized Berkeleyans taking a stand against the Vietnam War ("I-Feel-Like-I'm-Fixin'-To-Die").

ONE SUNDAY AFTERNOON
YARDBIRDS
COUNTRY JOE AND THE FISH
FILLMORE AUDITORIUM
OCT 23

## Revolution on Sunset Boulevard

In Los Angeles bands proliferated, but their identities stayed more separate than in San Francisco, for there was no cementing force like the hippie movement to bring them together. Here, everyone was an individual with individual inspiration and individual talent. Some groups stood out: the Doors (with Jim Morrison), for example, and Frank Zappa, Captain Beefheart ("Trout Mask Replica"), the bluesy Canned Heat ("Going Up the Country"), Steppenwolf ("Born to be Wild"), and Arthur Lee's Love ("Forever Changes").

The Doors, who debuted in 1966, took their name from Aldous Huxley's book *Doors of Perception*, consecrated to his experience with hallucinogens. Morrison garnered attention because of his provocative stage performance. More than a singer, he wanted to be a poet, a rebel, the conscience of a generation. Supported by solid musicians—notably organist Ray Manzarek, who was passionate about both jazz and composer Kurt Weill—Jim "the Lizard King" revived the myth of the rock and roll hero, fragile and triumphant, adored by hordes of fans but condemned to inevitable self-destruction. Of all the rock output in those crazy years, the music of the Doors is one of the rare examples to have survived to this day without suffering musically: "Riders on the Storm" and "LA Woman," for example.

The legend of Jim Morrison, singer for the Doors (album cover below), began to spread after his death in 1971.

## Zappa and His Mothers

Frank Zappa seemed very different. An erudite musician, he was subject to two major and apparently contradictory influences: black fifties doo-wop and composer Edgard Varèse. Zappa's favorite weapon was Dadalike humor, with references to Groucho Marx, whom he even resembled. Zappa understood that his audience was, like him, breaking its bonds with society. His musicians, the Mothers of Invention, like his entourage, reflected his aspirations. Through his albums Zappa developed the different facets of his inspiration, from the most complex *(Lumpy Gravy, Uncle Meat,* and the 1971 film *200 Motels)* to the most openly critical *(We're Only in It for the Money),* to the most frankly parodic *(Cruising with Ruben and the Jets),* performed in a fifties doo-wop style. Obsessed with the official recognition of his status as a contemporary classical composer, he performed the score to *200 Motels* with Zubin Mehta and the Los Angeles Philharmonic in 1970, and then saw Pierre

Frank Zappa (below), a prolific artist, tried everything: classical music and rock, film and video, and sometimes even politics. In the extravagantly produced *200 Motels,* his first feature film (in which Ringo Starr played the role of Zappa), Zappa cheerfully teased the narrow world of rock. For his third album, *We're Only in It for the Money,* Zappa received authorization from the Beatles to imitate the cover of their famous *Sgt. Pepper* album (below left).

# ZAPPA

Beneath a buffoonish look, Frank Zappa sustained a great interest in very serious music. After his *Lumpy Gravy* album, filled with nods to modern composer Edgard Varèse, Zappa explored a more jazzy vein in 1969's *Hot Rats* (shown here), accompanied by violinist Jean-Luc Ponty and Don "Sugarcane" Harris.

Boulez conduct a symphony orchestra performing his works in the mid-eighties.

## Lou Reed and the Velvet Underground

When Frank Zappa arrived in New York in July 1967 to set up his show of surrealist cabaret at the Garrick Theater, the local "underground" scene was already very strong. The *East Village*

*Other* newspaper drew artists with the same critical approach—notably directed against the Vietnam War, but with a less "erudite" musical orientation: the Fugs (with poets Tuli Kupferberg and Ed Sanders), the Holy Modal Rounders (with the young Sam

The Velvet Underground at the Dom in New York in 1967 (above), with a light show designed by Andy Warhol.

Shepard), Pearls Before Swine, and, a little more removed, the Velvet Underground.

Lou Reed also came from the field of poetry. His meeting Sterling Morrison and John Cale, highly trained in modern composition, determined the foundation of the Velvet Underground (a name taken from a sadomasochistic novel by Michael Leigh). The group's rough improvisations caused it to be banned from most clubs. Then pop artist Andy Warhol discovered them. The group rehearsed in Warhol's milieu, surrounded by Gerard Malanga's silkscreens, various superstars, and the actresses known as the Chelsea Girls—Ingrid, Viva, Ultra Violet, and Nico (who soon joined the group).

For several months the Velvet Underground performed at the Dom in New York's East Village. Warhol's hand was present even in the show's title—the Exploding Plastic Inevitable. Warhol "produced" the band's first album (*The Velvet Underground and Nico*, 1967), and, in fact, his presence

alone was enough to confer on it a certain aura that others were charged with transferring onto vinyl. The short period of the Velvet Underground (1967–9) profoundly marked pop music. Well after the band broke up, Lou Reed was still seen as the Chuck Berry of the eighties.

Andy Warhol's pop art manifested itself in all the activities of the Velvet Underground, such as, for example, the cover of its first album (detail, center). In the original version, which was released during the summer of 1967, this peel was removable and revealed the naked banana underneath. Today, collectors pay a fortune for this example of a fruitful collaboration between two artistic worlds.

Nico was a model-starlet when she met Andy Warhol. He made her one of the stars of his 1966 film *Chelsea Girls* and then suggested that Lou Reed entrust her with some vocals for the Velvet Underground. She participated in the band's first album before starting a solo career.

*Andy Warhol*

In 1968 rock and roll was at the heart of a vast cultural and political movement with its performers as its leaders. Rock served as a vehicle for the ideas of love, peace, and brotherhood that were being celebrated at giant festivals. But eventually it lost the biting sound that had made it inaccessible to many, and the music business took advantage of a larger and larger audience.

CHAPTER V
# THE VIEW FROM WOODSTOCK

The majority of the names that appeared on this poster for the Woodstock festival were relatively unknown to the general public before the concert. But the media impact of the event was such that in the blink of an eye a number of the artists became superstars. Big Brother and the Holding Company album cover (right).

Psychedelia made its official appearance in Great Britain in the fall of 1966, making an indelible mark on the musical world. The whole underground scene revolved around the magazines *IT (International Times)* and *Oz.* Concerts were organized in London at the Roundhouse, the Alexandra Palace, and a little club called the UFO. Two groups—Pink Floyd and Soft Machine—played there for the first time.

## Rock Goes "Cosmic"

Pink Floyd was led by an enraptured dandy, Syd Barrett, joined by three former architectural school students. With birdcalls, industrial noises, and

The members of Pink Floyd (above, at the end of the seventies) hid in the background of their stage productions. Over the years the stage show aimed more to seduce than to alarm. But when Syd Barrett (opposite) was in command in 1966–7, he plunged the audience into a climate of anguish far removed from the spirit of the "good vibrations" of the time.

blinding light shows, the Pink Floyd universe was like a nightmare, with science fiction as the excuse for all the theatrics *(The Piper at the Gates of Dawn)*. After Barrett's departure— he had become mentally ill—guitarist David Gilmour arrived and gave the music its "cosmic" style *(The Dark Side of the Moon)*. Pink Floyd was an influence on a number of groups.

Another band formed by students, Soft Machine, experienced a different fate. For the mods-become-hippies, the band was the realization of their old dreams of a modern jazz allied to pop culture. The name of the group—a superb underground reference—came from the title of a William Burroughs novel. Soft Machine was very popular in France, and in England the influence of the band's Robert Wyatt was considerable in the development of a progressive rock style; this style gradually separated itself from the traditional patterns of rock and roll. Wyatt left Soft Machine in 1971 after recovering

When Robert Wyatt left Soft Machine, he formed a new group, Matching Mole.

from a difficult album *(Fourth)* and founded the band Matching Mole. He reached the peak of his art in 1974 after a terrible accident that left him gravely injured. Supported by Pink Floyd, he recorded the album *Rock Bottom* (produced by the group's drummer, Nick Mason), at the time seen as one of the most original masterpieces in the history of rock.

Following the lead of the progressive, or art-rock, movement, the majority of new musical genres that proliferated in the seventies in Great Britain dawned between the end of

1966 and the end of 1968. The desire for change, for evolution, manifested itself in a 360-degree search for other sounds, other rhythms, other examples. The British empire was ready to provide a number, thanks primarily to India. In the 1965 song "Norwegian Wood," George Harrison had introduced the sitar to the music of the Beatles. The great Indian sitar player Ravi Shankar himself advised Harrison, particularly on the recording of *Sgt. Pepper* two years later.

Is *Sgt. Pepper* a masterpiece? A cornerstone in the history of rock? Or pure megalomania? *Sgt. Pepper's Lonely Hearts Club Band*, always a popular and critical success, opened the door to concept albums. After this time (1967) it was possible to spread out on one or more sides of a record in order to develop an idea or create a mini-opera. This genre triumphed in 1969 with the Who and its very ambitious rock opera *Tommy*. In the late sixties and early seventies, with operas and symphonies, rock flirted dangerously with a respectable classicism—the Moody Blues *(Days of Future Passed)*, Emerson, Lake and Palmer *(Pictures at*

Soft Machine, 1971 (above, on the cover of their third album). Left to right: Elton Dean, Hugh Hopper, Mike Ratledge, and Robert Wyatt. The apparent weariness reflects the tensions that were tearing the four musicians apart; Wyatt left the band a few months later. The humor, fantasy, and imagination then disappeared from the music of Soft Machine, yielding their places to an unsurprising jazz-rock.

*an Exhibition),* King Crimson *(In the Court of the Crimson King).* Everything was permitted ever since the Beatles, with the urging of their producer George Martin, had introduced violins here and a harpsichord there. They were often and quickly imitated by their cousins, the Stones *(Their Satanic Majesties Request).* Happily, there were still the blues.

## Supergroups, Megastars, Giant Festivals

By the end of 1966 the John Mayall–Graham Bond–Alexis Korner matrix had given birth to the first supergroup in history: Cream. The members were Eric Clapton (guitar), Jack Bruce (bass), and Ginger Baker (drums). With their high-volume rock-blues, they announced the intensification of the approach to rock, which later led to hard rock and heavy metal. The power trio had only one serious competitor: the Jimi Hendrix Experience.

Hendrix was American. He made his debut as a guitarist backing Little Richard and Curtis Knight, a rhythm and blues singer. During the summer of 1966, Chas Chandler (the former bassist for the Animals had become a manager) discovered him in a club in Greenwich Village, New York. He brought Hendrix to London and had him record a bluesy version of a standard, "Hey Joe," which was an immediate success. The music press was completely overwhelmed. There was now another guitar hero besides Clapton to carry out the fusion of the blues currents and psychedelia. Hendrix redefined the instrument, using all available effects to create previously unheard-of sounds. His influence was felt by every guitar player who followed.

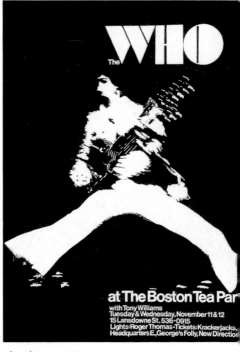

The WHO

at The Boston Tea Par

with Tony Williams
Tuesday & Wednesday, November 11 & 12
15 Lansdowne St. 536-0915
Lights: Roger Thomas · Tickets: Krackerjacks,
Headquarters E., George's Folly, New Direction

Valiant warriors of the British Invasion, the Who had a sullied reputation. They ended their concerts by destroying their instruments on stage, they wrecked their hotel rooms, and they threw their cars into their hosts' pools. In short, they constituted an extremely bad example for other groups—who hastened to imitate them.

In June 1967 Hendrix was one of the stars of the Monterey International Pop Festival in California. His performance remains a legendary moment in the history of rock concerts. Modest and unpretentious at first, this small festival was transformed by producer Lou Adler and John Phillips of the Mamas and the Papas into a showcase of California rock. Janis Joplin, the Jefferson Airplane, and Canned Heat were discovered there surrounded by Otis Redding, Ravi Shankar, and other key talents of the day. After Monterey the idea of more and more elaborate

Each of Jimi Hendrix's stage appearances threw the fundamentals of rock and roll into question. He "slayed" the electric guitar, like Charlie Parker "slayed" the saxophone. Performing after such giants was certainly not an easy task.

## Jimi Superstar

Jimi Hendrix was a larger-than-life figure, and all the festivals wanted to include him in their concerts. His guitar playing was enriched by new sounds, while remaining faithful to the spirit of the blues and its twelve-bar structure. His group, the Experience, underwent several mutations. His English back-up, bassist Noel Redding and drummer Mitch Mitchell, ceded their place to black Americans. His army buddy Billy Cox became bassist, and Buddy Miles, a drummer then much in vogue, joined them. The trio sometimes performed under the name Band of Gypsies. Hendrix hoped thus to reconquer the black audience. It was, however, a crowd of mostly white faces that acclaimed him at the festivals in Monterey in 1967 and Woodstock and the Isle of Wight in 1969.

## Janis Joplin

From 1966 Janis Joplin was a star of the rock scene in San Francisco. She was only twenty-three years old but already possessed a solid experience in the blues. Back in her native Texas, she'd grown up listening to the records of black artists, above all Bessie Smith. She knew Smith's songs by heart and managed to imitate them with a certain ease, but she could not have known that her destiny would be as tragic as her model's. In San Francisco the popularity of her group, Big Brother and the Holding Company, coincided with the growth of the hippie movement. She reigned at concerts at the Fillmore Auditorium and the Avalon Ballroom, but she lived alone, exploited by drug dealers and duped by her friends— the blues, always the blues. Discovered by Bob Dylan's manager, Albert Grossman, at the Monterey festival, she began a brief solo career which came to an end in 1970 in a motel with a fatal overdose. The legend was born. During the next decade, every female rocker would cite her as a model.

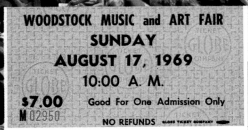

**WOODSTOCK MUSIC and ART FAIR**
**SUNDAY**
**AUGUST 17, 1969**
**10:00 A. M.**
**$7.00** Good For One Admission Only
M 02950
**NO REFUNDS** GLOBE TICKET COMPANY

gatherings developed, culminating at Woodstock (the Woodstock Music and Art Fair in White Lake, near Bethel, New York) in August 1969.

## Woodstock, Vision of History

More than 300,000 people flocked to attend these famous three days of music, peace, love, rain, and drugs. Little-known performers and groups (Richie Havens, Joe Cocker, and Ten Years After) found themselves propelled in one stroke to the level of megastars, due to the festival's highly promoted spin-offs (the film, live album, and tours).

The music business knew perfectly well how to profit from this fantastic publicity coup. Rock became an industry, with its constraints and its need for expansion. All the hype was successful. Suddenly a group did not count until it had appeared in a giant

The organizers of the Woodstock festival did not expect such a crowd, and they certainly did not expect that the majority of the spectators would enter without paying. Due to the general goodwill of the crowd there was no material damage or physical violence; this was not true of later events of the same type.

festival—the Isle of Wight or Watkins Glen or Toronto or Atchafalaya. Unlike Woodstock, these were like open-minded concentration camps that one entered for the simple pleasure of vibrating together to the faraway echoes of a patchwork of music ranging from jazz (Miles Davis) to Indian ragas (Ravi Shankar) to militant folk (Joan Baez) to modern funk (Sly Stone appearing at dawn on the stage at the Isle of Wight in blue fur boots). For such thrills, one was ready to hitchhike hundreds of miles, sleep in the rain, eat anything, be overcome by bad hash and warm beer, and wait for hours in a packed crowd patrolled by thugs with police dogs. These festivals of bliss sometimes ended tragically: While the Rolling Stones were playing in Altamont, near San Francisco, in October 1969, a man was killed by the Hell's Angels. The year ended badly.

## French Business

Was nothing going on in Paris that summer? While the United States and England knew joyous musical upheavals, Paris contented itself with rumors and copies so pale they bordered on caricature. Very few French artists, in fact, understood the reach of pop culture in the sixties. Ronnie Bird reflected the mod spirit of London in 1965. Serge Gainsbourg made himself an amused commentator. Nino Ferrer tried to be inspired by the Stax sound in imitative songs. Some clubs opened up to English rock, but on the whole, France remained far behind.

Then came May 1968, with its student protests. Suddenly French students could no longer stand just to hear about "swinging" London and "druggy" California—they wanted the same things in Paris.

Rock and roll, the favored means of expression, was one of the first beneficiaries of this awakening. Turning its back on Anglo-Saxon models, French pop music searched for new roots in folk music (Alan Stivell) or in several wild "revolutionary" groups (Komintern, Red Noise).

But everything fell apart, and in five years pop's destruction of French rock and roll reduced to almost nothingness the ferment from which had risen a legion of musicians. The absence of music classes and instrumental practice in the schools no longer favored the development of talent. As a consequence, the only musicians to survive the aftermath of May 1968 in France were those highly influenced by jazz.

In May 1968 Paris erupted with student protests. When the students took to the streets, shock troops were sent to gas and beat them. One outcome of this insurrection was the organization of a French concert and distribution network, all in the service of rock.

## Pop Music Triumphs

Internationally, excess affected every level of production: There were record-breaking crowds at concerts (150,000 people for a Led Zeppelin concert) and record-breaking album sales. New records of notoriety, through the use of hype. New records of destruction of hotel rooms (the Who, Led Zeppelin). New records for the ingestion of various substances, which would cause the death of several heroes (Brian

Jones in 1969, Jimi Hendrix and Janis
Joplin in 1970, Jim Morrison in 1971).
Always more, more, more.

IGGY AND TH

With the arrival of hard rock at the
end of the sixties, the record for volume
also fell. By the end of 1968 Blue Cheer
had a hit with Eddie Cochran's "Summertime Blues,"
and MC5 *(Kick Out the Jams)* and Iggy Pop and the
Stooges *(Fun House)* simply gave a more resonant
weight—in volume as well as in density—to the patterns
inherited from blues and rockabilly.

Led Zeppelin ("Stairway to Heaven") in England
continued the path traced by the Yardbirds: a hardened
blues sound with a heavy beat, embellished by
the virtuosity of its leader and guitarist, Jimmy
Page. The term "heavy metal" appeared to designate
a radical approach. Blues-rock at the beginning, the
music then tended more and more to favor the
effect of density and volume, climaxing with the
painful (for the eardrums) absurdity of Grand
Funk Railroad.

In the United States, however, the meeting of urban
hard rock with Southern blues generated the blossoming

Led Zeppelin (above,
Robert Plant and
the guitarist Jimmy Page)
could be considered the
first heavy metal group.
Initially inspired by
American blues
musicians, Jimmy Page
created a very complex
sonic universe. In
him the myth of the
"guitar hero" found
its full measure.

of groups like the Marshall Tucker Band *(A New Life)*, the Outlaws *(Lady in Waiting)*, Lynyrd Skynyrd ("Free Bird"), and, above all, the Allman Brothers Band *(Eat a Peach)*. The guitar playing of its leader, Duane Allman, who died in a 1971 motorcycle accident, influenced a number of artists, particularly his colleague Eric Clapton on "Layla." Further south, the Texas group ZZ Top ("Gimme All Your Loving") offered a heavier, strongly rhythmic approach to the blues. The tradition was inherited from various musicians on the Houston scene, including Lightnin' Hopkins, and was continued by flamboyant guitarists from Johnny Winter to Stevie Ray Vaughan.

James Osterberg, called Iggy Pop (below left and right), incarnated the radical and violent rock of Detroit. With the Stooges (a name taken from the Three Stooges) he disturbed late-sixties America, reminding it that the ghettos were burning and that its youth had no future.

## The Aftermath of Woodstock

In California the stars of the sixties realigned themselves into supergroups like Crosby, Stills & Nash, who were joined later by Neil Young *(Déjà Vu)*. In their wake a "Southern California" style appeared, reinforcing the myth forged by the Beach Boys. These records featured a laid-back atmosphere, polished production, and a return to folk inspiration blended with good old country music. It was a 100-percent American genre, occasionally fired up by songs bordering on parochialism (the Eagles'

1976 hit "Hotel California"). Even
Dylan rediscovered country and
performed with Johnny Cash
(*Nashville Skyline*, 1969). After
the psychedelic storm, America
searched for its roots and found
them in Nashville.

In perfect harmony with the
Southern California rock trend,
poetic and introspective songs
regained a large audience. Even if
they didn't use the rhythm or the
firepower of rock and roll, certain
singer-songwriters belonged to this
world in the late sixties and early
seventies. It was a question of attitudes, references,
and associations. Leonard Cohen *(Songs from a
Room)* and Joni Mitchell *(Blue)*, Tim Buckley
*(Greetings from L.A.)* and Paul Simon *(There Goes
Rhymin' Simon)*, Tom Waits *(Nighthawks at the
Diner)* and James Taylor *(Sweet Baby James)*—regardless
of their differences, their approaches, and their singing
styles—were recognized by the public as being part of
the same family. An identical movement developed in
England involving musicians searching for their roots in
Celtic tradition—the Incredible String Band *(5000
Spirits or the Layers of the Onion)*, Fairport Convention
*(Unhalfbricking)*, Pentangle *(Basket of Light)*.

Irritated by what they considered the general softening
of music, disgusted by the blaring sounds of the
triumphant progressive style (Supertramp, Emerson,
Lake and Palmer, and their by-products), and indifferent
to the exercise of virtuosity by jazz-rock musicians (the
Mahavishnu Orchestra), lovers of true rock and roll
worried about its survival.

## The Arrival of Decadence

After the weak musical trends of the seventies, rock
would regain its health, thanks to the proven remedies of
outrage, provocation, and surprise. The unexpected
appearance of the group Sha Na Na at Woodstock
foretold the future. Breathlessly, rock turned toward its

In 1973 no one
expected the arrival
of a group like the New
York Dolls (above).
The Dolls were a
pure product of New
York City's East Village,
with their cheekiness,
irreverence, and appetite
for provocation.
Their capacity for
playing vigorous,
bracing, and humorous
rock and roll on just
three chords inspired
dozens of "garage
bands"—small groups
from New York
neighborhoods. After
the Dolls' premature
break-up in 1975,
their guitarist Johnny
Thunders (opposite
left and right) carried
the flame of a
tattered dandyism.

roots, while at the same time carica-
turing them. At first this style of
music was intended as parody, but
the attitude became more serious
with the Flamin' Groovies
*(Teenage Head),* who re-created
the musical climate at the time of
the Beatles and the Rolling
Stones and established for
legions of small punk
groups the link between
sixties pop and the
minimalism of the
eighties. The decadent
New York Dolls *(Too
Much Too Soon)*—in
their makeup and
outrageous women's
clothing—caused a
surprise in 1973. Like
the Ramones a few
years later, this
archetypal "garage band"
—referring to its rehearsal
space—gave more
importance to a look
and attitude than to
musical exactitude.
It theatricalized
rock, as did
others—Alice
Cooper and
David Bowie, for
instance—with
much more
care and
technical
preparation.
A student
of the
British
mime

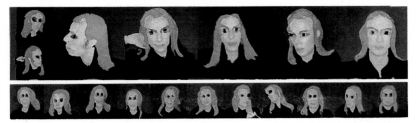

Lindsay Kemp, Bowie wanted to be an actor and singer. His carefully cultivated androgynous appearance shocked the world of rock used to the jeans of California musicians. Inevitably Bowie met Lou Reed, the other genius of provocation, and in 1972 Bowie produced Reed's album *Transformer,* which marked his great comeback after the Velvet Underground dissolved. Each in his own manner—Bowie's ode to Jean Genet and Reed's inventory of perversions at Andy Warhol's Factory—these two accomplices set the stage for a certain moral decay.

Seemingly more superficial, Bryan Ferry also played this game of affected decadence. After years of refusing the "look," he rediscovered the pleasure of sequined costumes and stage makeup when he played with Roxy Music *(For Your Pleasure).* Working close to Ferry for a short time was Brian Eno, who asserted himself as a dandy of the electronic age. His time with Roxy Music marked the appearance of the synthesizer in rock. Even he admitted that he was no musician, but he was a lover of experiments of all kinds, playing solo or in the company of other sound pioneers like Robert Fripp, Harold Budd, and, later, David Byrne. He would also work as a producer and was associated with Bowie, Kraftwerk, and U2, among others.

Just as extravagant but clearly more classical in their musical approach, Elton John *(Madman Across the Water)* and Marc Bolan of the band T. Rex *(Electric Warrior)* conferred a sort of panache on the glam-rock of the seventies. At that time theatrical rock productions were all the rage, as magnificently illustrated by Genesis *(Selling England by the Pound),* with Peter Gabriel and his numerous elaborate costumes.

From the first recordings of Roxy Music in 1972 to his later work without the band, Brian Eno (above) displayed remarkable command of the synthesizer, and his avant-garde experiments added another dimension to rock. His 1974 collaboration with guitarist Robert Fripp, like his later instrumental albums, was typical of a musical approach that could fit comfortably in the classical category.

Lou Reed (opposite center) and David Bowie (opposite below) were the two principal heroes of seventies glam-rock. They shared an innate sense of theatricality, understanding how simultaneously to shock and seduce their audience. Their collaboration was sometimes stormy, even though it produced a masterpiece like Reed's 1972 album *Transformer.*

By the middle of the seventies, rock had become too complex, too removed from its original beat, too convoluted. The packaging had become more important than the contents. In the face of excessively slick and expensive productions, small groups had no chance to find their place in the sun. Pushed by the need to revivify itself and rediscover its directness, rock sought refuge in the back of pubs. Once again the English scene came alive.

CHAPTER VI
## NO FUTURE?

English punk rockers (left) aggressively expressed their refusal of a society that offered them no prospects. Their slogan became "No future."

In 1975 it was possible to hear a band practically every night in London for the price of a beer at the bar. Music made a grand return to the wholesome values of rhythm and blues in the hands of groups like Ducks Deluxe *(Ducks Deluxe)*, Dr. Feelgood *(Malpractice)*, and Brinsley Schwarz *(Silver Pistol)*.

It did not take long for the excitement that reigned in the clubs to affect other spheres of musical production. Faced with the ill will of the big record companies regarding recording and promoting newcomers, groups seeking contracts gave rise to the creation of independent labels. Virgin Records made a fortune in 1973 with the synthesizer hit "Tubular Bells" by Mike Oldfield,

A computer operator in a cosmetics company, Declan MacManus—alias Elvis Costello—did not have to modify his appearance much to resemble Buddy Holly. With his fighting stance and nasty stare, in 1976 he tried to reintroduce the esthetic values of the fifties back into rock.

discovered Kevin Coyne and his warped blues, and resurrected Robert Wyatt, thanks to his wonderful *Rock Bottom.* More centered on pub rock, in 1976–7 Stiff Records brought together several angry young men such as producer/performer Nick Lowe, Elvis Costello, and Ian Dury, who, with his famous song "Sex and Drugs and Rock 'n' Roll," would be caught up in the punk explosion.

## The Birth of Punk

The word *punk* used to refer to a marginal person, a naïf, a victim of the adult world. In 1967 Frank Zappa used the term in reference to the hippies of San Francisco. At the beginning of the seventies, rock critic Lester Bangs invented the description "punk rock," which he associated with the "B" groups assembled by Lenny Kaye for the important double album compilation *Nuggets*. For many years these garage bands were the training grounds for the cream of American rock: brilliant soloists including Todd Rundgren (Nazz),

In the late seventies, Ian Dury (below) incarnated the spirit of pub rock, music based on rhythm and blues played against a background of free-flowing taps and a convivial atmosphere.

Leslie West (the Vagrants and Mountain), and Ted Nugent (the Amboy Dukes), as well as such marginal but influential legends as the Electric Prunes and the Thirteenth Floor Elevator.

In the United States the punk scene spread out from CBGB, a club in New York City's East Village. At the end of its long, dark, narrow room, local garage bands ground out a primitive, aggressive rock. The Velvet Underground, with its Warholian spirit, constituted one of the only two admissible reference points; the other, strangely enough, was French poetry: Patti Smith *(Horses)* and Richard Hell (and the Voidoids, *Blank Generation*) quoted

Rock and roll searched for references in cinema, literature, and the fine arts. The Velvet Underground took its name from a novel on sadomasochism (left) as a bohemian spirit wafted over the East Village of New York.

Rimbaud, and Tom Miller called himself Tom Verlaine. Their music as well as their attitude reflected the neoromanticism of a new Beat Generation, as it was dubbed by William Burroughs. Knowing they would lose from the start, they refused all hit-parade ambitions, wrapping themselves in a nihilistic, often self-destructive, attitude. Some would die, victims of drug overdoses. During this short period in the late seventies, rock again found its intensity, its flashes of craziness, and its urgency in the work, for example, of the Ramones, Blondie, and the Talking Heads.

CBGB's example would soon spill across America. Punk groups sprang up from the streets of Cleveland (the Dead Boys), Boston (the Modern Lovers), Los Angeles (X), and even San Francisco (the Dead Kennedys). Directly descended from the Velvet Underground, the Stooges, the Heartbreakers, and MC5, this explosion of urban rock was, among other things, a response to the general trend on FM radio of playing pop music that never surprised.

The exception to this trend was Bruce Springsteen, who succeeded by operating on an

# CBGB

## – PRESENTS –

**AMIN**

**DEAD ★ KENNEDYS**

**CRAMPS**

**URBAN**

**ALTER**

Punk rock installed itself in New York at CBGB in the East Village.

The Dead Kennedys along with Black Flag (posters above and below) represented the punk wave on the West Coast.

**BLACK FLAG**

'10 minutes' respite from the sanctuary of sleep'

at Mabuhay Gardens Wed. Oct 10 with **the Dead Kennedys**

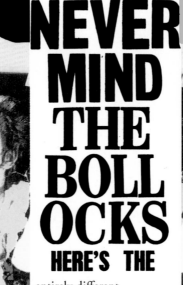

# NEVER MIND THE BOLL OCKS

## HERE'S THE

entirely different wavelength. The son of a working-class New Jersey family, Springsteen (nicknamed "The Boss") grew up on the outskirts of New York in the no-man's-land of Asbury Park. He retained the simple charm of an everyman, easily winning the hearts of the crowds who came to hear him play starting in the mid-seventies *(Born to Run)*. His rhythm-and-blues–soaked music, his emotional singing style, his lyrics recounting the daily life of the working class—halfway between social commentary and

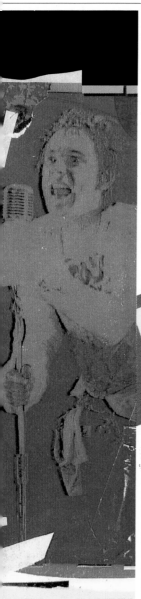

moral tale—and his ability to identify with a generation seeking justice and pride *(The River)* conferred on him a stature equal to Bob Dylan's ten years earlier. The comparison was unavoidable, though Springsteen never concerned himself with spirituality.

Springsteen led a "blue collar" movement that would include Bob Seger, Huey Lewis, and Southside Johnny (also from New Jersey), who reacted to an urban mechanized society in a virile way, sticking close to the roots of rhythm and blues. Through the years this style has become emblematic of American rock.

## England Discovered Punks

In 1975 Malcolm McLaren split his time between managing the New York Dolls, at the end of their career, and running his boutique on King's Road in London. He was motivated by the little-known but highly influential sixties philosophy of situationism (which saw art as action and cultural critique) and, like many others, grew tired of the greediness of show business and the new rock stars' mania for power. He wanted to launch a new group that would satisfy his taste for provocation and at the same time rediscover the raw energy and outrageousness of the pioneers of rock. In 1976 the Sex Pistols would personify his

John Lydon—alias Johnny Rotten (opposite and left)— was the leader of the Sex Pistols. His extraordinary stage presence threw the other musicians into the shadows. The only exception was the bassist, Sid Vicious, who succeeded in making a name for himself at the cost of self-destruction: He lacerated his chest with shards of glass, physically attacked the audience, was beaten up in return, swallowed all sorts of drugs, killed his girlfriend in a New York hotel, and finished by dying of an overdose in 1979. In two short years (1976–8) the Sex Pistols had succeeded in turning rock upside down and in bringing some of its fundamental values— outrage, theatricalized violence, defiance of the established order, and objection to the ideals offered up by their own culture—back into fashion. More than fifteen years later the punk-rock stimulus still disturbs and continues to make converts.

desires *(Never Mind the Bollocks Here's the Sex Pistols).*

What did it matter if Johnny Rotten and Sid Vicious could barely recognize a note of music? Shoplifters (found in McLaren's store!), riffraff, junkies, vandals, they were chosen because they looked like small-time thugs. Representing a marginal scene propelled forward by the media, they were the perfect antidote to the jubilee celebrations for the queen in 1977. A powerful trend developed, characterized in particular by self-destruction: pallid faces, torn clothes, pierced skin, shaved heads or hair glued into multicolored Mohawk crests. English punk turned its back on the elegance of such princes of pop as Elton John. Designers Vivienne Westwood (McLaren's partner) and Bernie Rhodes (manager of the Clash) transported the punk look into the world of fashion.

## IN THE U.K.

While the Sex Pistols were recording the reign of anarchy in the United Kingdom, the Clash (opposite) preached armed revolt. Joe Strummer (below right) was in part its brain, its "theorist." His group expressed the frustration of youth faced with a future of unemployment and police harassment in cities stricken by economic crisis. Through its songs and adoption of reggae protest tunes, the Clash also expressed solidarity with Jamaican immigrants in England.

Spirited and politicized, the Clash *(The Clash)* came on the scene in 1976 and was followed by hundreds of groups (like X-Ray Spex and Sham '69) who rediscovered rebellion, that fundamental quality of rock and roll. Even with little means and limited knowledge of music, each could get on stage, and the Roxy Club in London saw a long line of bands influenced by both the sixties and the punks: the Jam *(In the City)*, the Buzzcocks *(Another Music in a Different Kitchen)*, the Damned *(Damned, Damned, Damned)*, and the Gang of Four *(Entertainment)*. Small labels such as Radar, Rough Trade, and Sire flourished. But for this generation hit by economic crisis, the dismal observation of "no future" was the only response—quite a contrast to the positive and open ideas of the Woodstock generation.

### The New Wave

In 1978 the public wavered between the raw energy of punk nihilism and the ethereal, elegant, sophisticated music offered them at the same time by two new bands, the Police *(Outlandos d'Amour)* and Dire Straits ("Sultans of Swing"). Like Eric Clapton earlier on, the Police were influenced by Jamaican reggae as symbolized by Bob Marley, while Dire Straits explored a vein closer to the relaxed Southern rock practiced by J. J. Cale. Their almost immediate worldwide success reached several generations of listeners.

The recurrent tendency of rock to search for support from the largest crowd—obvious for simple commercial reasons—ended up creating concerts in gigantic stadiums where phenomena like Madonna flaunted themselves. Hypnotized, the media paid little attention to the fact that such artists obscured the intense wave of creativity

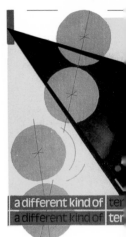

The Buzzcocks of Manchester recalled the Small Faces band of the mod era: ordinary kids in appearance, amphetamine-addicted rockers in reality. This sixties reference was not uncommon in the English new wave in 1977, as can be seen in the work of another group, the Jam.

that punk and new wave were producing in unexpected places.

When Ian Curtis killed himself in Manchester in 1980, his band, Joy Division *(Unknown Pleasures)*, was already the obligatory touchstone for the new wave movement. His music translated the gloominess of the modern world into an intense, emotion-charged atmosphere. The Cure, London suburbanites clearly haunted by the shadow of the poet Shelley, also laid claim to a somber romanticism. Sardonic, disillusioned offspring of the first punks, these groups contrasted sharply with the mainstream tendencies of the eighties: clear ambition and artificiality, with much more attention paid to cultivating a look than a musical signature (Duran Duran, Spandau Ballet).

In between, the arrival of the music video, largely broadcast by specialized cable channels like MTV, focused on physical appearance and stage settings. Musicians who were older—or less "cute"—were penalized, regardless of their talent. Some, like the fine English rhythm and blues musician Joe Jackson, rebelled against this conformity and the censorship in effect on

Robert Smith formed the Cure in 1978 in the London suburbs. One of the band's first songs, "Killing an Arab," was inspired by Albert Camus's *The Stranger*. These somber romanticists had numerous imitators who copied their attitudes, their clothes, and their hair.

The Irish group U2 (left) incarnated certain national values: passion, openness, idealism. Everything seemed to indicate that the term "heroic" was invented just to describe U2. The group received top billing at large charity concerts, on the same level as Sting, Peter Gabriel, and Bruce Springsteen. These artists brought a needed measure of soul back to rock and roll after years of indifference, frenzied ambition, and cynicism —indeed, of pure and simple nihilism.

television. Others shrewdly appealed to video and cinema to pass along their message. Thus, for example, Michael Jackson entrusted the creation of a short film for his 1982 song "Thriller" to Hollywood director John Landis. Without a doubt the film's success played a large role in the high level of record sales.

At the same time as the rock video, the compact disc turned the music business upside down. The successful reissues of back catalogue material reinvigorated overlooked groups and movements. Suddenly, rock turned its attention to the past, recycling it, not inventing much that was new. Obsessed with profits, the huge machinery of the music business wore out. Some promising groups were ground up by the star system, providing more alarming signs about rock's state of health.

## World Rock

But rock endures. Throughout its history, whenever inspiration was missing, people looked to old successful favorites. The Rolling Stones had adapted Chuck Berry and were copied in their turn by the Black Crowes, Telephone, and dozens of garage bands.

Today, the range of influence has drastically enlarged. Starting in 1965, when George Harrison brought the sitar to the music of the Beatles, musicians have learned to delve into popular music the world over. That search has conferred on rock a kind of new "world" dimension, as is clear in the work of musicians as far apart as Peter Gabriel, David Byrne, and Paul Simon.

Rock is in good shape, regardless of those who relentlessly predict its demise. Small labels are thriving and with them the hundreds of groups who are returning to the simple values of guitars connected to electricity. The politically conscious song has rediscovered its vigor and its audience through Tracy Chapman ("Fast Cars") and Sinéad O'Connor *(I Do Not Want What I Haven't Got)* and urban rappers. Current events offer a bottomless supply of issues to protest. After the disappearance of that intolerable disco music, so popular in the seventies, dance has recovered its place in "rave parties," spontaneous gatherings

around a booming bass sound. And now, after Memphis, Liverpool, and Manchester, there is a new focus: Seattle, with its "grunge" movement (Nirvana, *Nevermind*). Periodically victim of its own megalomania, rock always manages to rebound, drawing new strength from the inexhaustible reservoir of its audience. Elvis Presley can sleep peacefully: There'll be "Good Rockin' Tonight."

Rock has always been fascinated by new technology, risking the loss of its simplicity, warmth, and effectiveness. The icy synthesizers of the seventies and eighties happily gave way to the "samplers" (snippets of sound) of house music. Dance became an essential element again. Rap, funk, and its electronic cousin, techno-funk, enlivened "rave parties," improvised gatherings focused around a huge sound system and a disc jockey skilled at linking rhythms. The majority of these musical styles originated in the inner cities of America. All the rules were turned upside down, the music business exploded, and everyone managed to produce and distribute their music outside the traditional circuits.

Opposite and left: Illustration from a Kinks album cover.

Overleaf: Keith Richards of the Rolling Stones.

# DOCUMENTS

Supergroups, megastars, and giant festivals—the world of rock expresses itself in superlatives.

# Frankly Speaking

*When you give rockers the floor, they don't mince words. Those who are not specifically interested in promoting their latest album take the time to cast on their craft—and sometimes their colleagues— an eye as critical, frank, and direct as their music. It was not too long ago that the Beatles caused an uproar by stating that they were more popular than Jesus Christ: Insolence is also a fundamental quality of rock and roll.*

## The Truth About Rock and Roll

*Has rock and roll become too self-indulgent?*
No, I didn't say that. It is the interpretation that is too self-indulgent. We're led to believe that the music that was in fact simple and direct at the beginning was actually really complex and difficult. You can blame that on business, on the greed of some people, on the star system. There's an enormous gap between what things are and the way people perceive them.

People like me don't have a firm opinion on anything. I am just as stupid as the average guy. They pretend that I say things, but basically I do my job like everyone else. I write songs. Everyone knows more or less how that's done, OK? But

Iggy Pop.

they created this concept in the sixties. … I have been confined to this role, I have been pushed into this box for business reasons. However, the concept is false, completely false. But since nothing else exists, I do my best to live with it.

Van Morrison
*Les Inrockuptibles,* August 1989

## Rock and Roll Out of Jail

*What did your parents think at the time of the first Stooges albums?*
I think they were terrified, but they are very nice people who have never prevented me from doing what I wanted.

Oh, yes, one time, my father was really angry. We gave a concert in the city where he taught. I broke a bottle against my microphone stand and the glass flew in every direction. A shard cut a girl in the first row on the arm…. I had to get out of there quickly because the audience was going to lynch me. Later on, the cops nabbed me and brought me to the station. The next day, a local newspaper printed the court minutes of the incident. And everybody saw it, my parents' friends, my father—in short, the whole world. They held that against me. But he was a really good father. He got me out of jail when I was younger. He even came to my concerts.

Iggy Pop
*Les Inrockuptibles*
June 1990

### The Sex Machine Rolls On

"God got me in on the ground floor of every kind of music," [James] Brown exults backstage at Radio City Music Hall. "He put me into the game before Prince and Sly and Rick James and the Funkadelics. When—"

Instantly Brown cancels the thought and explodes with a torrential verbal outburst: "SEXMACHINEGOOD FOOTTHINKDOINGITTODEATH ICAN'TSTANDMYSELFWHEN YOUTOUCHMESUPERBAD COLDSWEATFUNKYCHICKEN INEEDYOURLOVESOBADBABY BABYBABY!"

He pauses, grinning ferociously, and spews it out again. The feat of precisely merged enunciation is doubly impressive on the second pass, the humming whole too specific to be psychobabble or doggerel filler, and yet not exactly a boast either. It's more of an involuntary mantra disclosure.

"Down in D.C. they talking about the go-go but I had them kids out in the streets while they were still babies, doing the popcorn with the Original Disco Man. Funk I invented back in the fifties. The rap thing I had down on my Brother Rapp (Part I), and you can check that. I enjoyed my thing with Afrika Bambaataa on Unity, but I did it more for the message than for the music. Michael Jackson, he used to watch me from the wings and got his moon walk from my camel walk—he'll tell you that if you ask. Same way, I was slippin' and slidin' before Prince was out of his crib; that's why Alan Leeds, who used to work for my organization, is on his management team, tipping and hipping him. I ain't jealous, I'm zealous. I ain't teased, I'm *pleased.* Who's gonna do James Brown better'n *James Brown?* Think!"

Timothy White
*Rock Lives,* 1990

## Rock and Roll: Too Much

It is totally a prisoner of its reputation and its myth. For me, life is much simpler if one forgets rock and roll a little. I draw the line there. I prefer that one speak of "Lou Reed music" as my subject. That way, there are no limits, no prohibitions, no "you can't do that," none of that blah-blah.… No one dares say that about a novel or a film, but as soon as the subject is a rock and roll record, everything is permitted.

Let's stop this imposture then.… Rock and roll is irrelevant.

*Is rock and roll totally empty now?*
All these definitions, they wear me out. Rock and roll is much too restrained for me. I don't like to feel enclosed. I write lyrics an adult can identify with. My new album, *Magic & Loss,* doesn't mean a thing to a kid. I don't write for kids. I haven't written for that audience since 1976. I always wanted to escape from the futility of rock lyrics. If I write, it is for adults to amuse themselves with a little bit of rock and roll, while listening to lyrics that engage them mentally.

Lou Reed
*Les Inrockuptibles*, January 1992

Lou Reed.

## Ice-T Thaws Out

*The rapper muses on past controversies.*

**RJ SMITH:** You go out of your way in interviews to say that you regret things you've said in the past about gay people. I wonder why you do that.
**ICE-T:** You know, you just grow up. Not just about gay people but about life. When you come from the kind of neighborhood I grew up in, masculinity is at a premium. The jungle creed says

the strong must feed on any prey at hand. That's just how it is. So everybody who is weaker than you, you say, "You're a faggot, sissy." It's not even based so much on sexuality, it's something on weakness. You looked on as weak. At some point, you say, "I thought being gay was something you choose to be." After further analysis, I feel that some people don't make a choice, it's a way they probably are born. You grow up and you learn, you don't just *know*. It's hard for someone who's brought up in a very masculine arena called the ghetto—it is an arena, you are thrown into this pit. Even people who aren't tough learn to walk tough.

I used to say things at our concerts

that were stupid. Like we'd say, "Everybody with AIDS be quiet." We didn't know what AIDS *was*. AIDS is serious. You die. I'm not beyond saying, yo, I'm wrong. But you gotta understand that everybody does not grow up in the same way.

My whole thing is: I'm straight. I don't even dig the use of the word *straight* because that says that somebody else is crooked. But I still don't totally understand it. Men kissing—I just don't totally understand it. But I think that's a little too much for you to ask of me. The same way that you might not be able to come into touch with some of the anger I have for the system. But I leave it at that. I ain't got anything to say about anybody gay. If that's your thing, cool.

**RJ SMITH:** Do you regret printing the lyrics to "Cop Killer" in the liner notes?

**ICE-T:** Well, in the new album we didn't put 'em in there. After you see your lyrics blown up 30 feet tall.… I know they can still transcribe the lyrics off the vocals, 'cause I rap real legibly, but I didn't print them on *Home Invasion* as a way of letting people feel censorship. Maybe one day we might have to have records where they come with a special decoder that will bring out the lyrics.

In a way, when we pulled "Cop Killer" it was a form of censorship. It's kind of good now, 'cause people come up and say, "Can I still get a copy?" And I'm like, "Nope." That's what censorship is like. It's a way of hitting you in the face when you can't buy it. Now the ones on the streets are turning into collector's items.

**RJ SMITH:** How much does "Cop Killer" sell for now?

**ICE-T:** They were selling it up in Santa Barbara for $300 if it's still sealed.

**RJ SMITH:** What about fans who say you're Ice-T and you're not supposed to back down to anybody?

**ICE-T:** I got to call my own shots. And they don't really know when it's a back down or when it's a retreat to return with superior firepower. You never know. You might say, "Oh, Ice-T backed down." But what good is me holding that record out there when I can't hit with another record? Warner Bros. wasn't going to back me on *Cop Killer 2* or *The Return of the Cop Killer*.

It wasn't really a form of weakness.

RJ Smith
"T-ing Off: This Time It's Personal"
*The Village Voice,* 13 April 1993

### Enya Expresses Herself

*The Irish singer's international hit "Orinoco Flow," on* Watermark *helped make her name as a soloist.*

Anything other than music is irrelevant to me. It is not that I am shielding myself or guarding myself.… I have no boyfriends, no hobby. Everything has had to be put aside while I have worked on my music. I believe you have only one chance to make a life and to do your work. That I have put first. That is why there is *Watermark*.… Almost all the music is played by me. It is recorded in real time. This is how we keep the music human. When we will perform live,…a real choir will sing with me as I play my instruments. This is my tradition. And I sing many songs in Irish because Irish is the language of my home and my friends. It is a language that expresses feeling much more directly than English.

Jim Fouratt
"Above the Watermark"
*Spin* magazine, May 1989

# John Lennon and the Beatles

*In 1973 John Lennon looked back on the phenomenon known as the Beatles. But he also had something to say about the present day.*

*Always the Beatles were talked about and the Beatles talked about themselves as being four parts of the same person.... What's happened to those four parts?*
They remembered that they were four individuals. You see we believed the Beatles myth, too. I don't know whether the others still believe it. We were four guys... I met Paul and said "You want to join me band?" you know. Then George joined and then Ringo joined. We were just a band who made it very, very big, that's all. Our best work was never recorded.

*Why?*
Because we were performers...in Liverpool, Hamburg and other dance halls and what we generated was fantastic, where we played straight rock, and there was nobody to touch us in Britain. As soon as we made it, we made it, but the edges were knocked off. [Manager] Brian [Epstein] put us in suits and all that and we made it very, very big. But we sold out, you know. The music was dead before we even went on the theatre tour of Britain....

*How would you trace the breakup of the Beatles?*
After Brian died we collapsed. Paul took over and supposedly led us. But what is leading us when we went round in circles? We broke up then....

*What was your feeling when Brian died?*
The feeling that anybody has when somebody close to them dies. There is a sort of little hysterical, sort of hee, hee, I'm glad it's not me, or something in it,

John Lennon. Right: The Fab Four.

you know? That funny feeling when somebody dies. I don't know whether you've had it, I've had a lot of people die on me. And the other feeling is What? What the f——! You know, what can I do? I knew that we were in trouble then. I didn't really have any misconceptions about our ability to do anything other than play music and I was scared. I thought, "we've f——in' had it."…

*How did Paul react?*
I don't know how the others took it. You can never tell…it's no good asking me…it's like asking me how you took it, you know, I don't know. I'm in me own head. I can't be in anybody else's. I don't know really what George, Paul or Ringo think any more than I do about, you know. I know them pretty well, but I don't know anybody that well. Yoko I know about the best. I don't know how they felt. It was my own thing. We were all just dazed.…

*Do you think you're a genius?*
Yes, if there is such a thing as one, I am one.

*When did you first realize that?*
When I was about twelve. I used to think I must be a genius but nobody's noticed. I used to think whether I'm a genius or I'm mad, which is it? I used to think, well, I can't be mad because nobody's put me away; therefore, I'm a genius. I mean genius is a form of madness and we're all that way. But I used to be a bit coy about it, you know, like me guitar playing, you know. If

there is such a thing as genius, which is just what…what the f—— is it, I am one, you know, and if there isn't, I don't care. I used to think it when I was a kid, writing me poetry and doing me paintings. I didn't become something when the Beatles made it, or when you heard about me, I've been like this all me life. Genius is pain, too. It's just pain.…

*What was it like, say, running around discotheques with the Stones?*
…We were kings and we were all just at the prime and we all used to just go around London in our cars and meet each other and talk about music with the Animals and Eric [Burdon] and all that. It was really a good time. That was the best period, fame-wise, we didn't get mobbed so much. I don't know, it was like a men's smoking club, just a very good scene.…

*And you feel the same way about rock and roll now at 30 as you did at 15?*
Well, it will never be as new and it will never do what it did to me then, but like "Tutti Frutti" or "Long Tall Sally" is pretty avant-garde. I met an old avant-garde friend of Yoko's in the Village the other day who was talking about one note like he just discovered that. That's about as far out as you can get. Even intellectually I can play games enough for reasons why that music is very important and always will be. Like the blues, as opposed to jazz, white middle class good jazz as opposed to the blues…the blues is better.…

*Because it's simpler?*
Because it's real, it's not perverted or thought about, it's not a concept, it is a chair, not a design for a chair, or a

better chair, or a bigger chair, or a chair with leather or with design… it is the first chair. It is a chair for sitting on, not chairs for looking at or being appreciated. You sit on that music.…

*Are you the Beatles?*
No, I'm not the Beatles. I'm me. Paul isn't the Beatles. Brian Epstein wasn't the Beatles, neither is Dick James. The Beatles are the Beatles. Separately, they are separate. George was a separate individual singer, with his own group as well, before he came in with us, the Rebel Rousers. Nobody is the Beatles. How could they be? We all had our roles to play…I don't believe in the Beatles. … I don't believe in them whatever they were supposed to be in everybody's head, including our own heads for a period. It was a dream. I don't believe in the dream anymore.…

*Who do you think is good today? In any arts…*
The unfortunate thing about ego-maniacs is that they don't take much attention of other people's work. I only assess people on whether they are a danger to me or my work or not.

Yoko is as important to me as Paul and Dylan rolled into one. I don't think she will get recognition until she's dead. There's me, and maybe I could count the people on one hand that have any conception of what she is or what her mind is like, or what her work means to this f——in' idiotic generation. She has the hope that she might be recognized. If I can't get recognized, and I'm doing it in a f——in' clown's costume, I'm doing it on the streets, you know, I don't know what—I admire Yoko's work.

I admire "Fluxus," a New York-based group of artists founded by George

Beatles fans were like no other.

Macuinas. I really think what they do is beautiful and important.

I admire Andy Warhol's work, I admire Zappa a bit, but he's a f——in' intellectual—I can't think of anybody else. I admire people from the past. I admire Fellini. A few that Yoko's educated me to... She's educated me into things that I didn't know about before, because of the scene I was in; I'm getting to know some other great work that's been going on now and in the past—there is all sorts going on.

I still love Little Richard, and I love Jerry Lee Lewis. They're like primitive painters...

Chuck Berry is one of the all-time great poets, a rock poet you could call him. He was well advanced of his time lyric-wise. We all owe a lot to him, including Dylan. I've loved everything he's done, ever. He was in a different class from the other performers, he was in the tradition of the great blues artists but he really wrote his own stuff—I know Richard did, but Berry *really* wrote stuff, just the lyrics were fantastic, even though we didn't know what he was saying half the time.

Jann Wenner,
*Lennon Remembers: The Rolling
Stone Interviews*, 1973

# Some Women Rockers

*Long confined to secondary roles—fans, groupies, backup singers—in the middle of the sixties female singers began to occupy center stage. One mostly remembers Janis Joplin. Hundreds of women rockers followed her example and have played the game as well as their male counterparts. Siouxsie, Patti Smith, and Madonna owe her more than a little something.*

## Janis Joplin

*Adored by hippies and Hell's Angels alike, Janis Joplin was more than a myth.*

Janis's Lyon Street apartment had a quaintly curved balcony that soaked up the rays of the afternoon sun. In the front room of the flat, which cost all of seventy-five dollars a month, Linda Gravenites slept on a large, comfortable couch and, by the great natural light of the day, did all her sewing. A tiny kitchen jagged off to one side of a large entry hall and in the back was Janis's bedroom, all dark and draped with the emblems of seduction, the final enrichment to Janis's image. Velvet and satin swathed her bed; her windows were veiled with lace and silk. One wall stood clear of sensuous enticement, its attraction a series of posters, Janis portrayed by her photographer friend Bob Seidemann. There were animals, always essential to Janis's happiness. A romping half collie named George enhanced the charm of the apartment; an aloof cat named Sam stalked possessively about. There were friends and laughter and Linda. All in all, it was, or should have been, the best year of Janis's life.

Rehearsals occupied the days, performances her weekend nights. Most of all, she had attained acceptance. She had trimmed down to a slight and attractive figure. She had acquired an aura, which, while not of a conventional beauty, had the irresistible radiance of energy. No longer an outcast, at twenty-four she was a queen, and if the regal chamber of her bedroom saw no permanence, wasn't she too young for that anyway, and wasn't her lofty status the reason, and didn't a revolving but continual solace to her flesh cushion the wilderness of her heart a little—just a little? Besides, what the hell, it was just one jazzy trick after another.

One day, just like any other day, Janis took George for a walk through the Panhandle. Resting on the grass for a while, she broke her boredom by throwing a stick for the dog to chase and return to her feet. Tired of the game, she pulled herself up and continued through the park, then stopped as a familiar figure came sauntering over the grass.

"Man, haven't seen you in ages!" Janis smiled.

"Yeah, long time. How's it going?"

Janis shrugged, going on to chat about her music and a number of other matters. "I need something new," she sighed.

"What've you been doing?"

Oh, this and...a little smack. I'm kind of strung out, though."

"What's it like?" Janis asked. "I've done it a couple of times, but I didn't like it, 'cause I always got really sick."

"Yeah," the girl nodded. "Well, I got sick the first couple of times too."

Janis peered at her curiously.

"The high's a groove, ya know...but it's a drag to be strung out. Listen, I gotta meet somebody. See ya around, right?"

Janis waved as she turned around to walk back in the direction of her apartment. George dipped his head toward her feet and pranced happily behind her as she headed home.

Myra Friedman,
*Buried Alive: The Biography of Janis Joplin*, 1973

Janis Joplin.

## Siouxsie

At a very young age she had shown the desire to go on stage and at sixteen had gone through several auditions… without success. The great turning point of her life was when she assisted for the first time at a Sex Pistols concert. She had become a member of the Bromley Contingent, that very special kind of fan club which accompanied Johnny Rotten and his friends everywhere. Outrageously made-up and clothed in sadomasochistic clothes—in savagely torn T-shirts, in bondage trousers, and adorned with all the paraphernalia of safety pins, zippers, and dog collars which supposedly conveyed a new "tragic feeling of life"—these boys and these girls rallied around the aggressive and minimalist music of the Pistols. They followed [the band] everywhere as faithful supporters, maintaining around them this climate of discontent and this aura of scandal, skillfully cultivated by Malcolm McLaren. Siouxsie paraded among them, her black hair cut very short and her eyelids painted in

mourning colors and wore, under an envelope of transparent plastic, underwear completely inspired by a fetishistic imagery. She had previously had the impression of being pushed to the background because she refused to be a female singer manipulated by men and obligated to sing "pretty songs." Now all at once, she felt she had gone through something new: "Until then I contented myself with waiting for something to arrive. And it came. Exactly at the right moment."

Marjorie Alessandrini
*Le Rock au Feminin,* 1980

## Patti Smith

You had heard of or read the name of Patti Smith here and there: She had published some short texts and record reviews (altogether rather banal) in *Creem* and *Rolling Stone.* Several collections of bizarrely fascinating poems appeared under her name: *Witt' Seventh Heaven,* with their references to Rimbaud, Brian Jones, and Mickey Spillane. The words, made to be very loudly read, chanted, spit out, howled, struck you with their rhythm. In the traditional American manner of the beat poets like [Allen] Ginsberg, this author and poet got on stage for recitations and lectures given in a loud voice. And one day—it was still at the beginning of the seventies—she began to be accompanied by a guitarist: Lenny Kaye, a rock critic friend who already had a background as a musician, having played the bass for various groups such as the Vandals and Man Ray. The passage was smoothed between the electric poetry and the rock and roll. Patti had a flaming passion, a violent energy, a dose of exhibitionism indispensable to every career of a star...and also, that not at all negligible quality, the profoundly American need to succeed, the desire to make it at any cost....

She also possessed the physical strength to succeed. Patiently made over the years, Patti applied herself to create in her body and her face the same energy and poetry as existed inside her. Everyone is born with the face and the body provided by nature. From there on, it's up to each person to play with it, to fashion it. Patti had behind her a history as a scrawny little girl, neither pretty nor ugly, a frustrated fan of Dylan and the Stones...who then, suddenly, one day moved with self-assurance onto the rock stage because she had finally become what she had dreamed! The pale intensity of her look and the sexual magnetism were both united in an extraordinary innocence. Her walk had the imprint of undeniable elegance and she modeled her look after Keith Richards: the hollow cheeks, the dark and tangled tresses, a certain rapid contraction of the facial muscles...and it was as if that sudden appearance of Patti Smith had been prepared by years of patient work on herself.

Marjorie Alessandrini
*ibid.*

## Madonna

*The last time we saw you in photographs, you were like Marilyn Monroe. It was like the image of a superstar, of a myth, and now all at once you've stopped all that.* Because I am like that. Because I like to go from one thing to the other. I like to show one facet, then another radically different one and make people understand that they're always

dealing with the same person. For me, it is essential. One time I had an important meeting with the head of Columbia. Well, he was an old man, a conservative type, and I arrived in fluorescent orange formfitting long johns and I had a little very low-cut tied blouse. He asked me if I wanted something and I said, "Yes, some popcorn." I began to eat it and it fell down my shirt and I picked it up from where it had fallen. The

problem of being a star is that you are placed straight away on a pedestal and that, from that time on, you no longer have the right to be a human being, to cry, to laugh at stupid things. That's the reason that I knock the image, so that people will reflect. I'm just a girl, that's all. I believe that people are surprised to see that I am intelligent and funny.

Marie Colmant
*Libération*, 14 May 1991

# Down Memory Lane

*Since 1955,* Billboard *magazine has published an annual list of top pop singles. Here is a look back at some milestones of the last four decades.*

### *Billboard*'s Pop Charts

Billboard *magazine's weekly rating of popular songs is determined by both sales and radio airplay.* Billboard *assigns year-end ratings to the top one hundred pop songs based on a complex formula that takes into account the number of weeks a particular song remained on* Billboard*'s pop charts and the various positions—1 through 100— the song attained on the charts from week to week.*

### 1955

1. "Cherry Pink and Apple Blossom White"
   Perez Prado

2. "Rock Around the Clock"
   Bill Haley & His Comets

3. "The Yellow Rose of Texas"
   Mitch Miller

4. "Autumn Leaves"
   Roger Williams

5. "Unchained Melody"
   Les Baxter

6. "The Ballad of Davy Crockett"
   Bill Hayes

7. "Love Is a Many-Splendored Thing"
   Four Aces

8. "Sincerely"
   McGuire Sisters

9. "Ain't That a Shame"
   Pat Boone

10. "Dance with Me Henry"
    Georgia Gibbs

## 1960

1. "Theme from *A Summer Place*"
   Percy Faith

2. "He'll Have to Go"
   Jim Reeves

3. "Cathy's Clown"
   Everly Brothers

4. "Running Bear"
   Johnny Preston

5. "Teen Angel"
   Mark Dinning

6. "It's Now or Never"
   Elvis Presley

7. "Handy Man"
   Jimmy Jones

8. "I'm Sorry"
   Brenda Lee

9. "Stuck on You"
   Elvis Presley

10. "The Twist"
    Chubby Checker

## 1965

1. "Wooly Bully"
   Sam the Sham & the Pharaohs

2. "I Can't Help Myself"
   Four Tops

3. "(I Can't Get No) Satisfaction"
   Rolling Stones

4. "You Were on My Mind"
   We Five

5. "You've Lost That Lovin' Feelin'"
   Righteous Brothers

6. "Downtown"
   Petula Clark

7. "Help!"
   Beatles

8. "Can't You Hear My Heartbeat"
   Herman's Hermits

9. "Crying in the Chapel"
   Elvis Presley

10. "My Girl"
    Temptations

## 1970

1. "Bridge over Troubled Water"
   Simon & Garfunkel

2. "(They Long to Be) Close to You"
   Carpenters

3. "American Woman/No Sugar
   Tonight"
   Guess Who

4. "Raindrops Keep Fallin' on My
   Head"
   B. J. Thomas

5. "War"
   Edwin Starr

6. "Ain't No Mountain High Enough"
   Diana Ross

7. "I'll Be There"
   Jackson 5

8. "Get Ready"
   Rare Earth

9. "Let It Be"
   Beatles

10. "Band of Gold"
    Freda Payne

**1975**

1. "Love Will Keep Us Together"
   Captain & Tennille

2. "Rhinestone Cowboy"
   Glen Campbell

3. "Philadelphia Freedom"
   Elton John

4. "Before the Next
      Teardrop
      Falls"
   Freddy Fender

5. "My Eyes Adored
      You"
   Frankie Valli

6. "Shining Star"
   Earth, Wind & Fire

7. "Fame"
   David Bowie

8. "Laughter in the Rain"
   Neil Sedaka

9. "One of These Nights"
   Eagles

10. "Thank God I'm a Country Boy"
    John Denver

**1980**

1. "Call Me"
   Blondie

2. "Another Brick in the Wall"
   Pink Floyd

3. "Magic"
   Olivia Newton-John

4. "Rock with You"
   Michael Jackson

5. "Do That to Me One More Time"
   Captain & Tennille

6. "Crazy Little Thing
      Called Love"
   Queen

7. "Coming Up"
   Paul McCartney

8. "Funkytown"
   Lipps, Inc.

9. "It's Still Rock and Roll
      to Me"
   Billy Joel

10. "The Rose"
    Bette Midler

**1985**

1. "Careless Whisper"
   Wham! Featuring
   George Michael

2. "Like a Virgin"
   Madonna

3. "Wake Me Up Before You Go-Go"
   Wham!

4. "I Want to Know What Love Is"
   Foreigner

5. "I Feel for You"
   Chaka Khan

6. "Out of Touch"
   Daryl Hall and John Oates

7. "Everybody Wants to Rule the World"
   Tears for Fears

8. "Money for Nothing"
   Dire Straits

9. "Crazy for You"
   Madonna

10. "Take on Me"
    A-Ha

**1990**

1. "Hold On"
   Wilson Phillips

2. "It Must Have Been Love"
   (from *Pretty Woman*)
   Roxette

3. "Nothing Compares
   2 U"
   Sinéad O'Connor

4. "Poison"
   Bell Biv Devoe

5. "Vogue"
   Madonna

6. "Vision of Love"
   Mariah Carey

7. "Another Day in Paradise"
   Phil Collins

8. "Hold On"
   En Vogue

9. "Cradle of Love"
   (from *Ford Fairlane*)
   Billy Idol

10. "Blaze of Glory"
    (from *Young Guns II*)
    Jon Bon Jovi

# The Twilight of the Stars

*Even stars die. Or else they fade away, suffering from alienation like everyone else. Brian Wilson, founder of the Beach Boys, underwent psychiatric treatment. Bob Dylan wore himself out with endless tours. Led Zeppelin closed up shop. But only their greatest moments will live on in our memory.*

## Brian Wilson

The [Beach Boys] made a name for itself thanks to its bittersweet vocal harmonies, which relegated the Beatles, on this point only, to the second rank. Like his teacher Phil Spector, Brian Wilson had invented new sounds: a zither combined with a baritone saxophone, mysterious percussion sounds falling in a cascade over a deep background sound....

All this music flowed from the heart of a twenty-four year old young man, introverted and melancholy, deaf in one ear since childhood and one who, according to the legend, had never dared step onto a surfboard.

Tired of incessant touring and pressure that never let up, Brian Wilson was a victim of a nervous depression at the end of 1964. He closeted himself away at home and didn't speak to anyone. For him it was the beginning of a phase of musical introspection which ultimately brought him, at the end of 1966, to the artistic summit of "Good Vibrations" and the album *Pet Sounds.* This record had already little to do with the exuberance which had made the Beach Boys famous: there was hardly a mention of hotrods or girls on the beach. Childhood had cast off its moorings, the wind had risen, a storm was brewing, and Brian Wilson stood on the edge of a pier, his eyes filled with tears.

Michka Assayas
*Libération*, 19 September 1988

## Bob Dylan

When one thinks of Bob Dylan, it is necessary to recall that Dylan has one point, one alone and it must be clear. "You lose yourself, you reappear, you discover suddenly that there is nothing to fear standing up alone, when a faraway voice, trembling, indistinct, and quivering, wakes you and forces you to listen…" ("It's All Right Ma").

That's the thrill, being woken by an indistinct voice only heard at the uncontrollable moment of a reappearance, real as a dream and in which his voice—his own voice—must

record, translate, and produce the echo. Dylan knows that when he sings there is no escape. In any case, he is caught between two fires that do not burn of the same matter, in the same way, or for the same reasons. There is no comfort in their light. The flames either lick too high or they blind him.

His only task, his only job is to make this trembling voice not absolutely disappear or not turn into the disquieting intimacy of his song. There is always, in a song that Dylan interprets by himself, the double sense of an invocation and of a revocation.

Daniel Dobbels
*Libération*, 31 December 1990

## Led Zeppelin

Jimmy Page's group was made up of John Paul Jones, John Bonham, and, of course, Robert Plant, whose shrill, dominating voice would put a stamp on a dozen albums. The Page/Plant couple would not delay in becoming a volcanic pair of young divorcés from Liverpool. Sprouting out of the blues roots which it never denied, Led Zeppelin became the champion of progressive, elaborate, belabored heavy rock (Deep Purple? Ha!), not hesitating, if needed, to play the role of sonic Marco Polos *(Physical Graffiti)*. Around 1975, the group was the sovereign of a realm built of huge bricks condemned to collapse under the weight of their omnipotence.

The end would be more abrupt. As with Keith Moon of the Who and Bon Scott of AC/DC, Led Zeppelin, one day in 1980, surrendered up its sacrifice to the rock legend: John Bonham was prematurely placed in his coffin. Deprived of the hammer of their stock, the surviving trio abandoned their position on high to several pathetic pillagers (like the band Kingdom Come) and stepped back from the fray in a manner befitting their rank. Page went astray. Jones tinkered about *(The Mission)*, Bonham had played on Friday the 13th *(Jason 2: The Return)*, and the great Robert rescaled the ramparts in June 1982 *(Pictures at Eleven)*. He would repeat the effort, with a somewhat faltering and devitalized heavy metal sound, on the next album and on average every two years, standing up to the attacks and challenges which the young mocking metal lackeys launched at him.

Gilles Renault
*Libération*, 22 May 1992

# Heavy Metal

*Hard rock has had a hard life.
Born twenty-five years ago with
the brilliant guitars of the
Yardbirds and their Holy
Trinity of Clapton, Beck, and
Page, it has become harder over
the years to see in it any of its
blues roots. How pleasurable it
would be to return to that less
heavily produced sound.*

### The Saga of Deep Purple

*At the end of the sixties the English
invented heavy metal, with its
bluesy strains.*

They were a supergroup whose imprint
would remain indelible throughout the
seventies—a key group, in fact, whose
avatars and metamorphoses (Ian Gillian
Group, Whitesnake, Rainbow) have
brought renown or still bring fame to
the world arena of heavy metal music.
The story of Deep Purple begins
roughly at the same time as that of Led
Zeppelin, in 1968. However at that
time, Jimmy Page's dirigible was well
ahead. While Led Zeppelin gave
hard rock its first masterpiece, Deep
Purple—organized around the pianist
Jon Lord and the guitarist Ritchie
Blackmore—confined itself to an
exclusive repertoire of pompously
arranged reprises in the wake of Vanilla
Fudge and the baroque rock of Nice.
This vaguely bastardized form of rock
taken from classicism was in fashion at
the end of the sixties. The first albums
of Deep Purple quickly established the
group on the English and, above all, the
American charts (more than a quarter
of a million albums sold in four months
in the United States!). On stage, these
somewhat stilted musical forms had a
tendency to blur a toccata in favor of a
sumptuous sonic massacre. Ritchie
Blackmore, a disciple of Jeff Beck,
slayed his amplifiers with great guitar
riffs, while Jon Lord played his organ in
the tradition of Keith Emerson in an
orgy of decibels.

Philippe Blanchet
*Heavy Metal*, 1985

Dee Snider (Twisted Sister).

## The Eighties

Current heavy metal has a thriving subgenre—even more extreme than most heavy metal—that is obsessed by death and destruction. The heirs of Judas Priest, [Ozzy] Osbourne's Black Sabbath, and other apocalypse-

Led Zeppelin.

Ritchie Blackmore (Deep Purple).

mongering heavy metal bands, cross-bred with the momentum and anti-pop ferocity of punk-rock, are the speed-metal or thrash bands of the 1980's. They bring portents of doom—personal and global—in words barked between jackhammer jolts of guitar, and they've become too popular to shrug off. Metallica...has sold a million copies of its latest album, ...And Justice for All, in less than a month; Anthrax's new State of Euphoria and Slayer's South of Heaven are also selling well.

Speed-metal has established its own musical and verbal conventions. More often than not, it pounds along at breakneck tempos, stopping and starting at irregular intervals like a fibrillating heart. It's anything but droning and hypnotic; its rhythms are choppy and memory-defying, calling for high-powered virtuosity and delivering new impact with every lurch.

Yet for all the tricky stops and starts, the harmonies are utterly simple. Most songs sputter along in every guitarist's first chord, E minor, and melodies are chanted or barked in a narrow range. So the music is both explosive and constricted—just the way a teen-ager can feel much of the time.

It's what speed-metal bands are saying, though, that gains them attention and notoriety....

A typical album includes songs about nuclear holocaust, dying in combat, captivity, turning into an automaton, going mad, about losing control and going on a rampage—tales of destruction, compulsion, power turned to evil ends, often envisioned in gory detail. There are also likely to be songs about outcasts and victims, the casualties of authority and power, along with denunciations of hypocrisy and assertions of independence. And some songs address suicidal feelings....

Some things are missing, too. Among them are love, romance, and sexuality; speed-metal bands don't sexualize violence the way slasher films or "Miami Vice" do. While there are accusations and pronouncements, there's very little moralizing....

[The] speed-metal bands add the defiance and anti-authoritarian sentiments that have always been a part of rock and roll. Their messages aren't demagogic commands to follow the leader or to go on destructive binges. They urge listeners to think for themselves, to insist on independence and the truth, to question authority and battle coercion....

[Rock] that tells teen-agers that they face a dangerous, irrational, brutal world tells them the unsanitized truth. It also tells each worried teen-ager that others have been terrified and enraged. ... [Speed-metal] bands strike a chord with millions of teen-agers because they reflect what's on their minds— and the songs tell them they are not alone.

Jon Pareles
"Speed-Metal: Extreme, Yes; Evil, No"
*The New York Times*
25 September 1988

### Metallica

Fans of intelligent music have to get used to it: Hard rock crops up there more and more. But be careful: When one says "hard" one is not just talking about the Scorpions, Dio, or other aging and largely FMized drudges, but the new wave of metal. This crowd of groups, from Soundgarden to Mary My Path passing through Faith No More, Prong, and White Zombies, have abandoned most of the grotesque cliches of the genre—skin-tight imitation leopard

Trust, a popular French heavy metal band.

leatherette pants, an assortment of faces of half-witted perverts, grandiloquent and obese albums— all benefiting a global approach favoring energy and brutal "efficiency," the hot air of the instrumental hemming and hawing, and nonsensical medieval dragon imagery. By way of distinctive omen, little remains today of these formula hard rockers but their basically cretinous lyrics and their long hair. All this in order to get to what? To Metallica, the missing link between hard and punk and the incontestable precursor of the metallic new age. Since 1983 this quartet of Americans based in San Francisco violently stated the foundations of speed metal with *Kill 'Em All*, their first album of noise with flourishes. At the beginning, their T-shirt–black jeans–sneakers style was identical to that of the international "kid" style and they were equally seduced by the slogans of "Kill Bon Jovi" and "More Beer." But their guitar work soon established the group as saviors of a dying metal style.

Metallica's recognition grew when they participated in the Monsters of Rock US tour two years ago where, performing between the Scorpions and Van Halen, they had no trouble calling attention to themselves as rising stars. Today, and without the help of radio, Metallica attracts complimentary articles—even in the very conservative *Rolling Stone.*

To get straight to the point, a Metallica concert is more than two hours of noisy energy as steadfast as it is invigorating. It is based on the (sexual) alternations between tension and hesitation and is played by the four heavy outlaws, who perform on an undecorated set consisting of stage curtains hanging in ruins over the amplifiers.

With only few rare "solos" there is a minimum of verbal exchange with the public, as if to ascertain that they're just among ourselves. On the whole, they pick up from the Ramones and from Motörhead but with a completely different set of references. As their 1987 mini-LP *Garage Days Re-Revisited* attests, the band remade in their unique style some songs by disappointing 1970s hard rock groups from Diamondhead to Budgie. We will have to seriously rethink this music— this usually cretinous music for

James Hetfield (Metallica).

morons served up by mental halfwits. Metallica is something different.... And their guitarist Kirk Hammett, seen backstage after the concert, is absolutely delicious!

Laurence Romance
*Libération,* 21 May 1990

# The Eighties

*After a chilly period marked by the "cold wave" and the domination of synthesizer groups, rock little by little heated itself up with the rediscovered simplicity of electric guitars.*

**Pygmalion and His Masterpiece**

*Quincy Jones produced the album* Thriller *by Michael Jackson.*

**Q:** Do you think that the success of Michael Jackson will help other black

INCLUDES THE SMASH HITS
I JUST CAN'T STOP LOVING YOU
BAD

artists in the United States?

**QUINCY JONES:** Each time that a black artist is recognized for his talent and his success, and that carves out a place for him within an industry—show business for example—it is a fundamental success for all blacks. Take the example of Michael Jackson, Richard Pryor, or Eddie Murphy: Their individual successes opened the path for other artists. That will create a new race of black directors, of black scriptwriters, of black actors. The fact that today Richard Pryor can with his name alone get a budget of $40 million for a film, for blacks it is the proof that everything is possible, and that gives them confidence and energy....

The success of Michael Jackson largely exceeds the framework of show business. He has galvanized all the black population. It is a political and social success. Don't forget that if blacks don't succeed more often, it is not because of a lack of talent—it is only because of the color of their skin. For the thirty years that I have been in the record industry, it has always been said that black performers could aspire to success on only a limited scale. Michael Jackson finally made the stereotypes fall. His sales figures have pulverized the economic givens of the market of the record industry, and at the same time that has pulverized the racism of certain black radio stations and of MTV. Each black person knows that he must be the best, and for that to happen, it is necessary that he extend himself. In succeeding, he will help all blacks to succeed.

Michele Halberstadt
*Libération*, 11 March 1984

## Grunge and Nirvana

**KURT COBAIN** *(Nirvana's vocalist and guitarist):* I'm from a white working-class family working in the logging industry. At home we ate a lot a macaroni and cheese. We weren't really poor but, all the same, at the bottom of the social ladder of the town. At least I could sleep more than I can now.

I had a marvelous, peaceful childhood. It was like in *Sesame Street.* … Jim Henson's puppets strongly influenced the imagination of kids of my generation, at the beginning of the seventies. It was an extraordinary program for kids, very innocent and even very educational: Through the puppets with their engaging personalities you learned to read and count. And even more, I had lots of great friends, and the family unit was very closely knit. It was a true gift from God, like a ray of sunshine every morning.

*Did you used to listen to what was going on on the radio or to harder American groups like MC5?*
At first, I listened to the Beatles and the Monkees, nothing else until I was ten years old. I didn't like at all what was on the only radio station we could get—the Carpenters and stuff like that. Then I followed my father into an even smaller community of loggers. There were guys older than me who smoked hash and

listened to Aerosmith, Black Sabbath, and Led Zeppelin. When my father was away, they got into the habit of coming to see me.… They only pretended to be my friends in order to screw their girlfriends on my father's bed, to booze it up, and to smoke.… But it was they who made me discover when I was only ten music as good as Black Sabbath, which I listened to religiously till about the time I was fifteen.

$K$urt Cobain (Nirvana).

*With the Clash, for example, did you understand that the punk-rock rebellion could convey something other than noise and power?*
What really changed my attitude, my idea of punk rock, was my first Black Flag concert. It was incredible. I was paralyzed and, at the same time, completely drawn to it with all my

being. It was simply the most extraordinary thing I had ever seen. There was this passion, this hatred, this energy that I understood that I could never make any other kind of music but that kind. That was in 1984.

Bates
*Les Inrockuptibles,* January 1992

## The Birth of "Rave"

At the dawn of the nineties…"rave culture" was born in England and spread through the rest of the world. It allowed each person—regardless of age, of social background, or of the color of their skin—to escape, for the space of one night, to where time stands still, to where the harrowing rules of reality which manage modern Western lives don't exist, and to where one could capture again the instinct of pleasure: to be together, tribally united by dance in the same vessel, rocked by the fantastic energy of the house. It is a music that, in functioning without or almost without "figureheads," has completely perverted the concept even of "stars," since they are no longer on the stage—empowered by the DJs—but on the floor.…

The whole house music sound arouses in its detractors the same incomprehension, the same reactions of slightly frightened rejection that punk rock and acid rock met in their time. The fear is that raves would essentially assemble an audience of druggies who would come together to dance till they dropped to a music that "just sounded all the same."

The criticism is obviously unjustified: From the garage sound to the ambient sound, from deep house to techno, house music is so varied in its conception that it offers exhilarating

possibilities to those desirous of mastering the machinery of their creative imagination.…

Laurence Romance
*Les Inrockuptibles,* March 1992

## Rock Rediscovered

As in Memphis and Liverpool not so long ago, rock blossomed outside the big cities in the eighties. In the United States, it was created around universities with their resources of radios, clubs, and record stores—the famous "college circuit."

The B-52s and REM were born on the campus of the University of Georgia in Athens. In Great Britain, Manchester was the center—it had always engendered excellent musicians (Graham Nash, Joe Cocker, the Buzzcocks, Lloyd Cole), and in a short period of time it became the mecca of new rock.…

More and more, rock turned inward and studied its past, adoring that which had burned brightly just a short time before. Through contact with other music, it crossbred, integrating all the invigorating contemporary black elements like rap and "house music" from Chicago. The exchanges went both ways: Prince and Michael Jackson had conquered the white audience with melodies and stage shows. They designed an image to seduce the audience, but without denying their closest influences like Jimi Hendrix and the Motown sound.

Today rock searches through its own history, mixing and remixing all that it has invented in forty years while waiting for the next revolution.

Alain Dister
September 1992

# The Surveillance of a Soul Rebel

*Years after Bob Marley's death, journalist Timothy White reveals how this hero to so many may have seemed a dangerous man to a powerful few.*

From steelpan to spooge, from mento to soca, the Caribbean Basin has always been a region steeped in topical music that could pierce the conscience just as surely as it could spark the spirit. And in Bob Marley's homeland, his music drew from the living heritage of those who had played and sung before him, to the point where his reggae became far greater than the sum of its influences. It grew from a cultural fad into a fierce act of faith and will, and then blossomed into a force of nature.

The Third World is most of the world, and by the time of his death in 1981 it was difficult to locate a corner of it where people had no knowledge of Bob and his message. But in Africa, it was impossible. From Nigeria, to Angola, to Zimbabwe, to Mozambique, to South Africa, his image and his music were carried through the streets by citizens struggling for freedom and self-determination, because he sang about and fervently supported the essential justice of all such movements. It's become fashionable since his passing to put a rigid political interpretation on Marley's outpourings, to label him a liberal of a particular cast, or a socialist, or even a closet Marxist. The facts do not support this conjecture. He had no dogmatic political beliefs....

At the time of the assassination attempt in Kingston on Friday, December 3, 1976, Marley was well on the way to becoming one of the best-known black figures of modern times....

Bob Marley was powerful politically, largely because he never codified or exercised any of his implicit power. Music was his life, and he had no hidden agendas. These are among the many reasons he may have been watched closely by eyes besides those of his admirers. And why those other eyes perhaps judged him a dangerous man.

There is no shortage of unanswered questions about the attempt on Marley's life. It's become well-known that Bob had enemies in the ghettos of West Kingston; Jamaican Labor Party (JLP) badmen in Tivoli Gardens and other strongholds of Opposition leader Edward Seaga were openly disgruntled that Bob seemed to be siding with Prime Minister Michael Manley's People's National Party (PNP) by consenting to appear at the upcoming PNP-sponsored "Smile Jamaica" festival. It's also known that Marley had inadvertently become involved in a fixed-race scandal at Caymanas Park Race Track.... When some of Marley's associates left the island with the loot ...Bob was the highly visible figure to whom the duped went for retribution. But there is the lingering theory that most of the internal and external political forces vying for control of Jamaica's destiny at this juncture were willing to let the chips fall where they may— providing they fell immediately and DECISIVELY. If a volatile, unbought figure like Marley should run afoul of his shantytown chums and become a martyr, the reasoning went, then so be it. If he never played another concert in Jamaica, that was okay too. But the bottom line was that he would be best out of the way. On one side of the mounting firestorm in West Kingston were jealous/overzealous PNP goons who had compelled Marley to appear at the Smile Jamaica concert; on the other side was gathered a distempered JLP-affiliated group of gravely disgruntled race-fixers from Tivoli Gardens.

The [JLP] gunmen came for Bob Marley in two white Datsuns on a Friday evening at approximately 8:45. ... Though wounded in the nighttime raid,...Marley went on to perform at the Sunday show. [Island Records head Chris] Blackwell made arrangements for a private jet to pick up Bob and friend Neville Garrick in a remote corner of Norman Manley Airport at 5:30 Monday morning. Bob was to remain guarded by plainclothes government security officials until he was safely aboard the plane....

However, when Bob and Neville awoke in the pre-dawn hours on Monday and began preparing to leave for the airport, there were NO security police to be seen.... Eventually, Neville and Bob had no recourse but to drive down the mountain, devoid of any police protection. They entered the closed Norman Manley Airport...and found their own way to the waiting jet. On the outskirts of the air field, a few soldiers in jeeps watched through binoculars but, curiously, kept their distance. Shaken and confused by the surreal setting, Bob and Neville gingerly crossed the tarmac, climbed aboard the aircraft, closed the door behind themselves and took off with the flight crew.

At roughly that same point, unbeknownst to Marley and Garrick, a confidential CIA/State Department telegram was moving on the government wires to the State Department in Washington, as well as to the American embassies in Kingston, Nassau and other Caribbean locations, offering a four-part synopsis of the ghoulish weekend developments in Jamaica. The communiqué's tagline: SUBJECT: REGGAE STAR SHOT; MOTIVE PROBABLY POLITICAL.

Timothy White, 1989

# The Record Column

*The first rock and roll recordings appeared on 45 rpm singles. The idea of an album occurred only much later with the development of high fidelity and more sophisticated recording techniques. Our selection brings together some now-historic albums, as they were chronicled in their time in the French monthly magazine* Rock & Folk.

## The Jimi Hendrix Experience: *Electric Ladyland*

This is a sound absolutely without equivalent in rock music. It's like the blues rooted forever deep in one's guts. The feeling of beauty and of outrageousness (and what can be more lovely than beauty, when it loses all boundaries?) The greatest rock guitarist in the world? Others say that there is someone else, but let us put aside these impossible rankings to plunge, all reason aside, into the strange universe of Jimi Hendrix. There are still very few people who could cut a double album without stumbling against the limits of their inventiveness and without spinning in circles. Still fewer among them are those who can create. Hendrix has created thirteen works (and the three others so profoundly carry his imprint...) that they could only be his. With this record, he confirms himself as the equal of the Beatles and Dylan....

Maybe anxiety is an indispensable element in making good music. Certainly, Hendrix is a lunatic, a survivor scarred by life, an obsessed destroyer of beauty and an intoxicated searcher of an inaccessible paradise. He is a superb scratcher of guitars and of internal wounds, and for him a dream is the exact opposite of a refuge. Masochism? More likely a vital and mortal necessity for a man who knows (or senses?) that if he reaches serenity, there will not remain anything more for him to say. This record illustrates strongly the Hendrixian paradox: He (Hendrix) must, without flagging, destroy the man he is in order to get to create his art. And that art, like a vampire, nourishes itself on the stability of the man and leads him inescapably

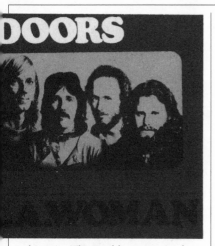

to his ruin. The terrible process in the painful birth of beauty. It is nothing to regret since the artist lives only in function of his work and he only dies for it; deprived of this (or of the means of continuing it) he would also be necessarily led to die—more quickly perhaps—but in any case without satisfaction.

That is why men like Jimi Hendrix cannot do otherwise but burn up their lives: The more intense the fire, the more beautiful the creation. Thanks to those artists of the stature of Jimi Hendrix rock music has acquired new dimensions, beyond the disgusting insipid sentimentalities, frenzied plagiarisms, and rhythms without substance we currently hear.

Rock lives.

Philippe Paingaux
1968

### The Doors: *LA Woman*

The most beautiful rock album that the Doors have ever recorded. It is always questionable enough to speak in elegiac terms about the last album of an artist who has just died. There are too many examples of these critics who, the day after the death of a star, believe themselves obligated to see in the last recording that the artist had created the masterpiece of his career—thus making *Cry of Love* the "best Hendrix." When Hendrix died, he became "Jimi," and his wildest detractors took the opportunity to come and whimper about "his tragic fate." *LA Woman* is, I repeat, the best rock album that the Doors have recorded. It is absolutely true.

Musically, *LA Woman* is a return to roots: For example, in "Been Down So Long" the music quotes, in its stunning progression, a loud and heavy blues like the "Crawling King Snake" of John Lee Hooker. Rhythm and blues is also present in "The Wasp" and "The Changeling" where Krieger provides a magnificent demonstration of his talents at the wah-wah pedal. And then there is "Love Her Madly," typical of the Doors, and the two splendid morsels, the truly poignant "Riders On the Storm" and "Hyacinth House."

The most striking thing, and that which entirely pervades this record, is that it serves as evidence of the cohesion of the Doors: Nothing here is tentative. The piano and organ parts of Ray Manzarek grow considerably richer, giving the group a more filled-out sound on which Morrison "sets" his enormous voice. He has never sung so well. Morrison—the most cannibalistic among you will not miss the opportunity to carefully search the contents of *LA Woman* in order to find in it the "signs" and the "proofs" of Morrison's imminent end. They will be found. The leader of the Doors had been Death's companion for such a long time and Morrison did not hesitate to speak of it.

Yves Adrien
1971

## David Bowie: *Aladdin Sane*

Bowie's approach is always intellectual. This latest album, *Aladdin Sane,* proves it more perhaps than any other. Bowie's music should always be listened to ironically. Here it is a confrontation of contemporary attitudes with neo-fifties accents, cabaret revival, but also a Cecil Taylor–like piano. But Bowie's "musical intelligence" reaches such a degree of perfection that the music of *Aladdin Sane* never seems like a series of collages

or an amalgam. To the contrary, it constitutes an important contribution to the new rock and roll esthetic.

There is nothing whorish or vulgarly easy in this sequence of the works. Instead, the musical whole presents an ambitious sonic approach. If "Watch That Man" is in the tradition of *Ziggy Stardust*, with "Aladdin Sane" and "Time," Bowie takes a new step in his sonic research. Thus Mike Gargon's

piano echoes Mick Ronson's guitar in the Yardbirds. For "Lady Grinning Soul," the sentimental accents disappear into a clear modern approach in their utilization of sounds. Moreover, Bowie remains an extraordinary chronicler of rock, showcasing in his lyrics all of the legend, all of the history of this music. "Panic in Detroit" is an homage to the great era of John Sinclair's White Panther Party. There are also the precise references to the world of "decadent" stars in "Cracked Actors," which is very similar to Lou Reed's lyrics, for example. "The Prettiest Star" is an old song written at the same time as *Space Oddity* and serves as the transition between "Time" and a very personalized version of the Stones's "Let's Spend the Night Together." There again, the romantic quality disappears in a wild but controlled din.

The pleasure of this album is subtle: There are no disruptions. Bowie succeeds, in essence, to place side by side in *Aladdin Sane* songs like "Time" and the already famous "Jean Genie" in a manner which seems at ease. *Aladdin Sane* has the ambition to prove that Bowie is more than a phenomenon of fashion but a true "synthesizer-creator" of the seventies. Who could pretend that he has not succeeded, except those for whom the blues did not exist before the Stones, those for whom there had never been an Elvis Presley before the Beatles? Bowie is a genius, like all the greats of rock.

Paul Alessandrini
1973

## Bruce Springsteen: *Born to Run*

Springsteen has already made two records, two dense and juicy confessions, somewhere between the

rage of Bob Seger and the poetic élan of Tim Buckley. *Born to Run* only keeps the essential words and the brilliance of phenomenal rage which is his voice.

It's a little like the sound in *Before the Flood,* but in a totally different timbre, more naturally large and deep. Dylan and Springsteen have only temperament and sensuality in common. *Born to Run* is an unexpected gift, a gift not only of great rock and roll but, above all, a gift of the wonderful fellow the music reveals. It's as if Dylan had a brother who sang in a harder fashion but who was not a copy of Dylan. There will never be another Dylan; old Bob is sufficient. Springsteen is there, moaning words, syllables, and phrases and then suddenly bellowing toward a black sky. The band sounds mercilessly huge, but the organ and piano parts alternate with subtlety and the magnificent saxophone chorus flashes out as if, at that precise instant, one truly had the need for the lofty splendor of a saxophone. All the songs are of the same flesh and blood, the blood of a wolf. Sometimes full and direct, like "Born to Run" and "Night," sometimes

grandiose and fearsome ("Backstreets" and "Jungleland"), these are motorized ballads like Mott the Hoople could never drive. And Springsteen mutters his fantasies ("Meeting Across the River") and his passions ("She's the One," an extraordinary song where all the gestures are like torture) in the frightening manner of a drunken tightrope walker who is a little too amorous, but so strong that he crushes you all at once with a huge guitar riff and drinks you in with his smile. The album must have been recorded in a garage. Yes, it is really the appropriate sound for this music, a large garage and the noise of the devil. And three microphones on stage, all for him, even though he runs and even though his loud voice is superb. For all those who climb the walls when the night descends, be happy, Bruce Springsteen is for you. The rest is only dust.

François Ducray
1975

## Joy Division: *Unknown Pleasures*

A band for neurasthenics, people whose most intense occupation consists of—

with few exceptions—interesting themselves closely in Death and in Peter Hammill. Let us go on. Since mid-1979, Joy Division had been the strongest antidote to the "musical valium" (as Elvis Costello notes in "Strict Time") which threatened, week after week, to anesthetize us permanently. *Unknown Pleasures* persuades us that all is not lost, that there are still people who will fade away from laziness and that the misery strenghens the spirit. Truth be told, *Unknown Pleasures* remains a most exhilarating record. The voice of Ian Curtis and "Disorder" comes out with a humble and involuntary vigor. Veiled, frightened, strange, it seems terrified of the body it inhabits. "Disorder" and its repetitive, overwhelming, untamed riffs, is the product of a band who would have survived anything, heirs to a chaotic, invertebrate world no longer managing to stay upright except by a discipline, by a hopeless asceticism.

In this battle against a world which has crumbled, Joy Division triumphs with a ferocity and an unpredictable jubilation. The dense and claustro-phobic texture of *Unknown Pleasures* is essentially due to the astounding work of Martin Hammett. Instead of cutting away each instrument to work at its strength, he proceeded by a series of implosions into turning the sound towards the inside. Echoes to infinity, layers of indecipherable instruments. Hammett, a true crazy man, has invented the most human sound of the decade. Call it industrial or psychedelic, it is the sound which all the world will try to imitate for a good while. And all that will remain will be Joy Division.

Michka Assayas
1979

**Sex Pistols: *Never Mind the Bollocks Here's the Sex Pistols***

Finally. It's been such a long time.... Such a long time for what? It's difficult to explain: I've heard a lot of good records in the last ten years and a reasonable number [of good ones] are released each year, but this time it's... truly different. We don't give a damn whether the Pistols are punk or something else. Forget about that. The only thing that counts is that they are the Pistols. Not only do they stand head and shoulders above the best groups of the new wave (which is beginning to be the holy dumping ground for fashionable ghosts), but above all they are unique. Johnny Rotten is the most charismatic personality to appear on the rock scene for a long time.

He is also an extraordinary (in the most exact definition of the term) singer. His unique phrasing, this manner of drawing out words, of cutting them off with what you think is a smile—this voice which one could call a bleat, if it were not so triumphant, would make him an absolute innovator.

But he is much more than that. He is terribly real. He is not a dupe either of the punk nonsense or of the star trip which is awaiting him, and he lives each word of his songs. The words of the Pistols are important, but in the manner of real rock lyrics: they only make complete sense in their context. This aggression, this rage, have we accumulated so much frustration?

The shiver that possesses the listener to these Pistols has one meaning; rock and roll finds in it suddenly something new—neither explicit or explainable, of course. It carries the impalpable sense of the era, 1977, the time of [the German terrorist group] Baader-Meinhof, and it is not a coincidence. The strange romanticism of a desperate hope… Eleven songs (they appear in a different order in the English version and are completed by a twelfth, "Sub-mission"). It is difficult and useless to make a choice: None of them let up on the implacable intensity of the ensemble.

This record allows no chance. Listening to two sharp sides is incredibly exhausting, it empties all energy, confronts a too visceral and total truth to be explained here. Don't make Rotten a hero or a star—this record must be a personal experience, it can only be that. And you can't ignore it. In any case, I hope that for you.

Hervé Muller
1977

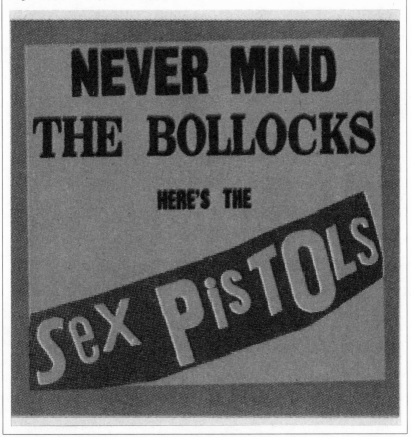

# Discography

*Following is a list of recommended albums to expand upon each chapter's text. Record labels—in a constant state of flux—have not been included; an album is best identified by its artist and title.*

## CHAPTER I

Charles, Ray, *His Greatest Hits*

Cochran, Eddie, *The Eddie Cochran Singles Album*

Crudup, Arthur, *The Father of Rock and Roll*

Domino, Fats, *Million Sellers by Fats*

Haley, Bill, *From the Original Master Tapes*

Holly, Buddy, *Complete*

Howlin' Wolf, *Moanin' in the Moonlight*

Johnson, Robert, *Complete Recordings*

King, B. B., *The Best of B. B. King*

Lewis, Jerry Lee, *Classic*

————, *18 Original Sun Greatest Hits*

————, *Live at the Star Club*

Orbison, Roy, *The Legendary Roy Orbison*

Perkins, Carl, *Original Sun Greatest Hits*

Presley, Elvis, *The Complete Sun Sessions*

————, *A Golden Celebration*

Vincent, Gene, *Gene Vincent and His Blue Caps*

Waters, Muddy, *Down on Stovall's Plantation*

Williams, Hank, *40 Greatest Hits*

## CHAPTER II

*Back to Mono* (anthology produced by Phil Spector)

Berry, Chuck, *Chess Box*

*Best of Doo-Wop Ballads*

*Best of Doo-Wop Uptempo*

Les Chaussettes Noires, *100% Rock*

Cooke, Sam, *Live at the Harlem Square Club*

Darin, Bobby, *Ultimate Bobby Darin*

The Drifters, *All the Greatest Hits and More*

Everly Brothers, *The Everly Brothers*

Hallyday, Johnny, *Le Twist*

Little Richard, *The Specialty Sessions*

Nelson, Ricky, *Legendary Masters Series*

The Platters, *Magic Touch*

Wilson, Jackie, *Mr. Excitement*

## CHAPTER III

The Animals, *Best of the Animals*

The Beatles, *The Beatles' Second Album*

————, *Meet the Beatles*

————, *Revolver*

————, *Rubber Soul*

Beck, Jeff, *Beck-Ola*

————, *Truth*

Brown, James, *Dance Machine*

Franklin, Aretha, *Lady Soul*

Gaye, Marvin, *What's Going On*

The Hollies, *All-Time Greatest Hits*

The Kinks, *Kinks*

————, *You Really Got Me*

Mann, Manfred, *The Best of Manfred Mann*

Morrison, Van, *Astral Weeks*

Redding, Otis, *Otis Blue*

The Rolling Stones, *Aftermath*

————, *Big Hits—Vol. 1 (High Tide and Green Grass)*

————, *Rolling Stones Now!*

————, *12 x 5*

The Who, *The Who Sell Out*

————, *The Who Sings My Generation*

Wonder, Stevie, *My Cherie Amour*

The Yardbirds, *For Your Love*

## CHAPTER IV

Baez, Joan, *Farewell, Angelina*

The Band, *Music From Big Pink*

The Beach Boys, *Pet Sounds*

————, *Surfin' USA*

Big Brother and the Holding Company, *Cheap Thrills*

Brown, James, *Live at the Apollo*

Buffalo Springfield, *Buffalo Springfield*

The Byrds, *The Byrds' Greatest Hits*

————, *Mr. Tambourine Man*

The Doors, *LA Woman*

————, *Strange Days*

Dylan, Bob, *Blonde on Blonde*

————, *Bringing It All Back Home*

————, *Highway 61 Revisited*

The Four Tops, *Anthology*

Franklin, Aretha, *Aretha's Gold*

————, *Young, Gifted and Black*

Gaye, Marvin, *What's Going On*

The Grateful Dead, *Live Dead*

———, *Workingman's Dead*

The Jefferson Airplane, *Surrealistic Pillow*

Ochs, Phil, *I Ain't Marchin' Anymore*

Robinson, Smokey, and the Miracles, *Anthology*

Ross, Diana, and the Supremes, *Anthology*

Sam and Dave, *An Anthology of Sam and Dave*

Simon and Garfunkel, *Wednesday Morning, 3 AM*

The Temptations, *Anthology*

The Velvet Underground, *The Velvet Underground and Nico*

———, *White Light/ White Heat*

Wonder, Stevie, *Stevie Wonder's Greatest Hits*

Zappa, Frank, *Hot Rats*

———, *Uncle Meat*

**CHAPTER V**

The Allman Brothers Band, *At Fillmore East*

The Beatles, *Sgt. Pepper's Lonely Hearts Club Band*

Bowie, David, *Aladdin Sane*

———, *The Rise and Fall of Ziggy Stardust and the Spiders from Mars*

Canned Heat, *The Best of Canned Heat*

Cohen, Leonard, *Songs From a Room*

Cream, *Disraeli Gears*

———, *Fresh Cream*

———, *Wheels of Fire*

Creedence Clearwater Revival, *Bayou Country*

———, *Green River*

Derek and the Dominos, *Layla*

The Eagles, *Desperado*

Eno, Brian, *Before and After Science*

The Flying Burrito Brothers, *Gilded Palace of Sin*

Gainsbourg, Serge, *Aux Armes, etc.*

Genesis, *The Lamb Lies Down on Broadway*

Green, Al, *Let's Stay Together*

Hendrix, Jimi, *Are You Experienced?*

———, *Axis: Bold as Love*

———, *Electric Ladyland*

King, Carole, *Tapestry*

King Crimson, *In the Court of the Crimson King*

Led Zeppelin, *Led Zeppelin*

———, *Led Zeppelin II*

Mayall, John, and the Bluesbreakers, *Turning Point*

MC5, *Back in the USA*

———, *Kick Out the Jams*

Mitchell, Joni, *Court and Spark*

Morrison, Van, *Moondance*

New York Dolls, *Too Much Too Soon*

Newman, Randy, *Twelve Songs*

Pink Floyd, *More*

———, *The Piper at the Gates of Dawn*

Ramones, *Ramones*

Reed, Lou, *Transformer*

The Rolling Stones, *Exile on Main Street*

———, *Sticky Fingers*

Roxy Music, *Avalon*

Sly and the Family Stone, *Stand!*

Soft Machine, *Third*

Springfield, Dusty, *Dusty in Memphis*

The Stooges, *Fun House*

———, *Raw Power*

The Who, *Tommy*

———, *Who's Next*

Wonder, Stevie, *Talking Book*

*Woodstock*

Wyatt, Robert, *Rock Bottom*

Young, Neil, *After the Gold Rush*

**CHAPTER VI**

The B-52s, *The B-52s*

Bashung, Alain, *Oh Gaby*

Black Flag, *Damaged*

Blondie, *Parallel Lines*

The Clash, *The Clash*

———, *Sandinista!*

Costello, Elvis, *King of America*

———, *This Year's Model*

The Cramps, *Songs the Lord Taught Us*

Culture Club, *Color By Numbers*

The Cure, *Pornography*

Dead Kennedys, *Fresh Fruit for Rotting Vegetables*

De La Soul, *Three Feet High and Rising*

Dire Straits, *Brothers in Arms*

Funkadelic, *One Nation Under a Groove*

Guns 'n' Roses, *Appetite for Destruction*

Hell, Richard, and the Voidoids, *Blank Generation*

*Indestructible Beat of Soweto* (compilation)

Jackson, Joe, *Look Sharp!*

Jackson, Michael, *Off the Wall*

———, *Thriller*

The Jam, *All Mod Cons*

John, Elton, *Madman Across the Water*

King Sunny Ade, *Juju Music*

Kuti, Fela Anikulapo, *Original Sufferhead*

Ladysmith Black Mambazo, *Shaka Zulu*

LL Cool J, *Mama Said Knock You Out*

Lynyrd Skynyrd, *Street Survivors*

Madonna, *Like a Prayer*

Marley, Bob, *Babylon by Bus*

———, *Burnin'*

Metallica, *...And Justice for All*

Motörhead, *No Remorse*

N'Dour, Youssou, *Immigrés*

Nirvana, *Nevermind*

O'Connor, Sinéad, *I Do Not Want What I Haven't Got*

Parker, Graham, *Howlin' Wind*

Pearl Jam, *Ten*

Pere Ubu, *Dub Housing*

The Police, *Reggatta de Blanc*

The Pretenders, *The Pretenders*

Prince, *Purple Rain*

Public Enemy, *It Takes a Nation of Millions to Hold Us Back*

Public Image Ltd, *Second Edition*

Queen Latifah, *All Hail the Queen*

The Ramones, *Leave Home*

The Red Hot Chili Peppers, *Blood Sugar Sex Magik*

R.E.M., *Document*

———, *Lifes Rich Pageant*

Rita Mitsouko, *C'est Comme Ca*

The Rolling Stones, *Some Girls*

Run-D.M.C., *Raising Hell*

The Sex Pistols, *Never Mind the Bollocks Here's the Sex Pistols*

Simon, Paul, *The Rhythm of the Saints*

Smith, Patti, *Horses*

Sonic Youth, *Daydream Nation*

Springsteen, Bruce, *Born to Run*

———, *The River*

Stiff Little Fingers, *Inflammable Material*

Talking Heads, *Remain in Light*

Television, *Marquee Moon*

Thompson, Richard and Linda, *Shoot Out the Lights*

U2, *Achtung Baby*

———, *The Joshua Tree*

Waits, Tom, *Rain Dogs*

X-Ray Spex, *Germ Free Adolescents*

Young, Neil, *Rust Never Sleeps*

# Filmography

*American Graffiti*, dir. George Lucas, 1973

*The Decline of Western Civilization*, dir. Penelope Spheeris, 1981

*The Decline of Western Civilization Part II: The Metal Years*, dir. Penelope Spheeris, 1988

*Don't Look Back*, dir. D. A. Pennebaker, with Bob Dylan, 1967

*Gimme Shelter*, dir. the Maysles brothers, with the Rolling Stones, 1970

*The Girl Can't Help It*, dir. Frank Tashlin, with Fats Domino, the Platters, and Little Richard, 1956

*A Hard Day's Night*, dir. Richard Lester, with the Beatles, 1964

*The Harder They Come*, dir. Perry Henzell, with Jimmy Cliff, 1973

*Help!*, dir. Richard Lester, with the Beatles, 1965

*The Kids Are Alright*, dir. Jeff Stein, with the Who, 1979

*King Creole*, dir. Michael Curtiz, with Elvis Presley, 1958

*The Last Waltz*, dir. Martin Scorsese, with the Band, 1978

*Monterey Pop*, dir. Albert Maysles, D. A. Pennebaker, and others, with Jimi Hendrix, Otis Redding, Janis Joplin, and others, 1969

*Rude Boy*, dir. Jack Hazan and David Mingay, with the Clash, 1980

*Sid and Nancy*, dir. Alex Cox, 1986

*The T.A.M.I. Show*, dir. Steve Binder, with the Rolling Stones, Chuck Berry, James Brown, and others, 1965

*This is Spinal Tap*, dir. Rob Reiner, 1984

*Tommy*, dir. Ken Russell, music by the Who, 1975

*Woodstock*, dir. Michael Wadleigh, with Jimi Hendrix, Joe Cocker, Country Joe and the Fish, and others, 1970

*Yellow Submarine*, dir. George Dunning, with the Beatles, 1968

# Further Reading

Bane, Michael, *White Boy Singin' the Blues: The Black Roots of White Rock*, Da Capo, New York, 1992

Bangs, Lester, *Psychotic Reactions and Carburetor Dung*, Knopf, New York, 1987

Charles, Ray, and David Ritz, *Brother Ray: Ray Charles' Own Story*, Da Capo, New York, 1992

Christgau, Robert, *Christgau's Record Guide: The '80s*, Pantheon, New York, 1990

DeCurtis, Anthony, and James Henke, eds., *The Rolling Stone Illustrated History of Rock and Roll*, third edition, Random House, New York, 1992

Escott, Colin, *Good Rockin' Tonight: Sun Records and the Birth of Rock and Roll*, St. Martin's, New York, 1991

Friedman, Myra, *Janis Joplin: Buried Alive*, Crown, New York, 1992

Frith, Simon, *Sound Effects: Youth, Leisure, and the Politics of Rock 'n' Roll*, Pantheon, New York, 1981

Gillett, Charlie, *The Sound of the City: The Rise of Rock and Roll*, Pantheon, New York, 1984

Guralnick, Peter, *Feel Like Going Home: Portraits in Blues and Rock 'n' Roll*, HarperCollins, New York, 1989

————, *Lost Highway: Journeys and Arrivals of American Musicians*, Borgo, San Bernardino, California, 1991

————, *Sweet Soul Music: Rhythm and Blues and the Southern Dream of Freedom*, HarperCollins, New York, 1986

Hebdige, Dick, *Subculture: The Meaning of Style*, Methuen, London, 1979

Hopkins, Jerry, *Elvis Presley: A Biography*, Simon and Schuster, New York, 1971

Hopkins, Jerry, and Daniel Sugerman, *No One Here Gets Out Alive*, Warner, New York, 1985

Marcus, Greil, *Mystery Train*, Dutton, New York, 1990

Marsh, Dave, *Born to Run: The Bruce Springsteen Story*, Dell, New York, 1981

Murray, Charles Shaar, *Crosstown Traffic: Jimi Hendrix and the Post-War Rock 'n' Roll Revolution*, St. Martin's, New York, 1991

Nite, Norm, *Rock On: The Illustrated Encyclopedia of Rock 'n' Roll*, HarperCollins, New York, 1985

Norman, Philip, *Sympathy For the Devil: The Rolling Stones Story*, Linden Press, New York, 1984

Rolling Stone Press, *The Ballad of John and Yoko*, Doubleday, 1982

————, *The Rolling Stone Encyclopedia of Rock & Roll*, Pareles, Jon, and Patricia Romanowski, eds., Summit, New York, 1983

Shelton, Robert, *No Direction Home: The Life and Music of Bob Dylan*, Ballantine, New York, 1987

Stern, Jane, and Michael Stern, *Elvis' World*, Knopf, New York, 1987

Szatmary, David P., *Rockin' in Time: A Social History of Rock and Roll*, Prentice-Hall, Englewood Cliffs, New Jersey, 1987

Thomson, Elizabeth, and David Gutman, *The Lennon Companion: Twenty-Five Years of Comment*, Schirmer, New York, 1988

Tosches, Nick, *Hellfire: The Jerry Lee Lewis Story*, Delacorte, New York, 1989

Ward, Ed, et al., *Rock of Ages: The Rolling Stone History of Rock & Roll*, Summit, New York, 1986

Wenner, Jann, *Lennon Remembers: The Rolling Stone Interviews*, Penguin, New York, 1973

Whitcomb, Ian, *After the Ball: Pop Music from Rag to Rock*, Limelight, New York, 1986

White, Timothy, *Rock Lives: Profiles and Interviews*, Holt, New York, 1990

Zappa, Frank, *The Real Frank Zappa Book*, Simon and Schuster, New York, 1989

# List of Illustrations

# Index

# Photograph Credits

# Text Credits

Writer and photographer Alain Dister was born in Lyons, France, in 1941. His written work has always focused on rock and roll, and he is the author of many books and articles on the subject. His photographs (which span a variety of themes) have been exhibited in museums and galleries around the world, and he has produced a number of music shows for French television.

*For Elise and Marie-Hélène*

Translated from the French by Toula Ballas

Project Manager: Sharon AvRutick
Typographic Designer: Elissa Ichiyasu
Assistant Editor: Jennifer Stockman
Design Assistant: Penelope Hardy
Text Permissions: Neil Ryder Hoos

Library of Congress Catalog Card Number: 93–70487

ISBN 0–8109–2831–0

Copyright © 1992 Gallimard

English translation copyright © 1993 Harry N. Abrams, Inc., New York, and Thames and Hudson Ltd., London

Published in 1993 by Harry N. Abrams, Incorporated, New York
A Times Mirror Company

Printed and bound in Italy by Editoriale Libraria, Trieste